Too Good To Be True:
James Collinsworth and the Birth of Texas

(1802-1838)

By
Roy S. Newsom, Jr. and James B. Collinsworth, Jr.
2012

Published by Westview, Inc.
Kingston Springs, Tennessee

PUBLISHED BY WESTVIEW, INC.
P.O. Box 605
Kingston Springs, TN 37082
www.publishedbywestview.com

© 2012 Roy S. Newsom, Jr. and James B. Collinsworth, Jr.
All rights reserved, including the right to reproduction in whole or in part in any form.

ISBN 978-1-937763-75-6

First edition, November 2012

Photo credits: Photo of James Collinsworth; Courtesy State Preservation Board; Austin, TX; Accession ID: CHA 1989.419; Photographed by Eric Beggs 1/12/96, post conservation. © State Preservation Board (2010), Austin, Texas. All rights reserved, including further reproduction, commercial display, incorporation into other works, or conversion to digital media.
Other photos provided by the authors.

The authors have examined each citation in this book in light of the principle of fair use of a copyrighted work and believe that our citations comply with that principle. The citations used in this book provide facts about real individuals in the 1750-1850 time period. Although each fact comprises a very small part of the cited work, when aggregated and interpreted, these facts reveal significant accomplishments by historical characters and related cultural developments in that period, making the public more aware of the awesome nature of its past and heightens its interest in further study.

If any copyrighted material has been included not in compliance with fair use, proper credit will be inserted in future printings, if any, after notice has been received.

Printed in the United States of America on acid free paper.

Thank You

The authors wish to acknowledge
the encouragement,
research assistance and financial
support in publishing this book
generously provided by our
"Collinsworth Cousins."

William Raymond Clark and wife Claudia
Al Collinsworth and wife Susan
Chris Collinsworth and wife Kelly
Gloria Newsom Huggins and husband Fred
Charles Newsom and wife Jo
Tom Newsom and wife Marilyn

We also wish to thank our wives,
Deborah (Jim) and Nancy (Roy),
for your support and encouragement
throughout this entire process:
for your patience during our research trips
to archives, libraries, museums and historic sites and
for being "abandoned" at home
while we were glued to a computer
searching, emailing and writing.
Thank you!

Contents

Chapter 1 – A Family of Courage and Determination 1

Chapter 2 - Growing up in Antioch 7

Chapter 3 – Antagonists and Friends 11

Chapter 4 – The President Appoints an Attorney 21

Chapter 5 - Stirring Up Flames of Revolution 53

Chapter 6 – Birth of the Republic of Texas 61

Chapter 7 - The Battle of San Jacinto 81

Chapter 8 - Commissioner to the United States 95

Chapter 9 – Wealth and Fame at Last 109

Chapter 10 - Good News Gives Way to Bad 121

Chapter 11- Death of a Dream . . . then a Man 135

Chapter 12 - Probate Reveals an Insolvent Estate 145

Chapter 13 - In Memoriam 155

Index 159

James Collinsworth as a young attorney.[1]

---

[1] Kimbrough Dunlap, a descendant of Benjamin Franklin Collinsworth and an early Collinsworth researcher, in a letter to James B. Collinsworth, Jr. dated November 29, 2000.

Chapter 1 – A Family of Courage and Determination

The story of a man's life begins well before his birth. A major factor which shapes him, one over which he has no control, is his ancestry – his DNA. So this story of the life of James Collinsworth begins with a brief look at his parents and grandparents.

Father - Edmund Collinsworth

James' father, Edmund Collinsworth, was born and raised in Virginia. Edmund's mother, Barbara Fox, was married first to Major John Cockrill[1] who died shortly after the birth of their son, also named John. Young John Cockrill was given a new father through the marriage of his mother to David Collinsworth in about 1759.[2] Edmund was born to David and Barbara about 1760.

In March of 1777, while still a teenager living in Virginia, Edmund and his brother John enlisted in the First Virginia Regiment commanded by Col. George Gibson and served as a private in Capt. William Hoffler's Company.

---

1. Granville Goodloe, William and Mary Quarterly, Vol III 1894-1895, p 69.
2. Sarah Foster Kelley, West Nashville. . Its People and Environs, (Nashville), p 11.

After the defeat of the Revolutionary Army at Brandywine that allowed the British to occupy Philadelphia, Gen. George Washington decided to establish winter quarters in December of 1777 at Valley Forge, Pennsylvania, so he could keep watch on the British army without exposure to surprise attack. The First Virginia Regiment joined Gen. Washington at Valley Forge that December and spent the harsh, deadly winter there, alongside about 12,000 other soldiers. Housing was overcrowded, food shortages were acute and many soldiers were poorly clothed and undernourished. Illness kept many from duty. Nearly 2,000 American soldiers died of disease.[1]

Edmund's military training began in earnest as winter passed. In February of 1778, former Prussian officer Baron von Steuben arrived in camp and introduced a tactical training strategy. He drilled soldiers into an effective fighting force.

That June, the army departed Valley Forge pursuing the British as they evacuated Philadelphia. They also encountered the retreating British Army at Monmouth Court House on June 28, 1778. After other skirmishes, Edmund went back to Virginia and remained with his company through April, 1780 for a service of three years.[2]

In 1783 Edmund and his brother John were each granted 100 acres of land in Nelson Co. KY, near Bardstown.[3] By 1792 Edmund had claimed his land and by 1793 he had sold it to move to Nashville, where he was reunited with his half-brother, John Cockrill.[4]

The first record of Edmund's presence in Nashville identifies him as a private in Nash's Company, Isaac Roberts' Regiment of the Militia, Territory South of the Ohio, 1794.[5] In October of 1795 Edmund and Robert Thompson, his soon-to-be brother-in-law, along with 19 others were appointed patrollers or searchers, Robert in Capt. Shannon's Company and Edmund in Capt. Parks Company.[6]

---

[1]. National Park Service http://www.nps.gov/history/logcabin/html/vf.html Accessed 3/3/2011.
[2]. National Park Service http://www.nps.gov/history/logcabin/html/vf.html Accessed 3/3/2011.
[3]. Willard Rouse Jillson, *Old Kentucky Entries and Deeds*, (Louisville: The Standard Printing Co., 1926), p 324.
[4]. *"First Census" of Kentucky, 1790*, (Washington: Heinemann-Brumbaugh, Washington, from extant Tax Lists of all counties existing in 1790), p 22.
[5]. Virgil D. White, *Index to Volunteer Soldiers 1784-1811*, (Waynesboro, TN: The National Historical Publishing Co., 1987), p 132.
[6]. Carol Wells, *Davidson Co. TN County Court Minutes 1792-1799*, (Heritage Books, Inc.), p 92.

Chapter 1: A Family of Courage and Determination

Mother - Alice Thompson Collinsworth

James' mother, Alice Thompson Collinsworth, was born in Ireland in a section called Ulster, probably County Antrim, near the city of Belfast.[1] Her parents were James and Elizabeth Thompson and her siblings at her birth were Alexander, Catherine, and John. James and Elizabeth decided a better life awaited them in the new world. As was the custom for poor emigrants, James probably contracted to work for a ship owner for a few years as payment for his family's voyage. Their fifth child, Robert, was born in transit from Ireland.

After about three months aboard the ship, they arrived in Delaware Bay and sailed up the river to Philadelphia in the colony of Pennsylvania. They settled near Philadelphia, probably in Lancaster or York County and stayed there for several years. While there, Elizabeth had another baby, this time a girl she named Elizabeth, after herself.[2]

About 1778 James received word from his relatives Abselom, Charles, Andrew and Elijah Thompson, who were living in a remote frontier settlement called Watauga, on the west side of the big mountains in Washington County, North Carolina. The message was that a band of settlers would be leaving from Watauga for French Lick, as Nashville was known then, on the Cumberland River where each man would receive a square mile of land, 640 acres, just for going there to settle. So James and his family left Pennsylvania traveling by foot and on horseback along the 'Great Road' from Philadelphia through the Shenandoah Valley of Virginia to Watauga, a distance of over 400 miles. It is not known how long James and his family were with their relatives in Watauga before they all prepared to venture deeper into the wilderness.

John Egerton in *The Faces of Two Centuries 1780-1980*[3] describes the grueling journey from Watauga to French Lick: By the first of November 1779, General James Robertson had assembled a company of people anxious to move to French Lick. Between 200 and 300 younger men and boys started the 500 mile journey through the Cumberland Gap on the Wilderness Trail with pack horses, food, provisions and the colony's assorted herd of livestock.

Soon after Robertson's party had left to go by land, John Donelson organized a flotilla of flat bottom boats to set out, transporting the older men, the women and children, the servants, and most of the household belongings of the settlement along a crooked river path on the Tennessee, Ohio and Cumberland Rivers.

---

[1]. *Texas Society DAR Roster, Vol. IV.*
[2]. William Bruce Turner, *The Turner Family*, (Nashville: Parthenon Press, 1960), pp 8-9.
[3]. John Egerton, *The Faces of Two Centuries 1780-1980*, (Nashville: PlusMedia Incorporated, 1979), p 16.

Although General Robertson's party started out with no women or children among them, the party was joined by many families along the Wilderness Trail. They traveled, not in close ranks, but widely scattered along the trail. By the time the bleak chill of December came, the party numbered close to 400. James and Elizabeth were about 45 years old and their children ranged from about 20 down to 14 years of age during this journey.

The winter of 1779-1780 was one of the coldest on record, but in spite of the bitter cold there was a constant trickle of settlers to the Cumberland Country. When the party arrived on December 25, 1779, it was very, very cold, so cold that the Cumberland River was frozen over and they were able to lead the livestock across the river on foot.

In January 1780 Donelson's flotilla began their arduous river journey down the Holston, into the Tennessee, up the Ohio and finally up the Cumberland River. On May 1 men from the eight stations met at The Bluffs and adopted the Cumberland Compact. James Thompson, his son Robert and their relatives were among the 256 signers of the historic document.

By 1790 James Thompson built a new chink-and-daub log cabin on his 640 acres near Richland Creek, southwest of Nashville. On February 25, 1792 young Alice Thompson felt something bad was about to happen. In her own words:[1]

> *I was blessed with a knowledge of presentment of danger so I was looked to as an adviser in the little settlement. That day I told Mrs. Caffrey, "we must hurry up and finish our work, we are going to have trouble today." She said "what is it to be?" I told her "the Indians are going to make a raid on us today."*

As the evening approached James Thompson went to the woodpile to chop and bring in firewood for the night. A bright, glowing wood fire was the one luxury they could afford. He chopped his firewood, and carried it by great armfuls and threw it over the yard fence. As he was stacking it near the door a party of twenty to thirty Creek Indians, who were awaiting this opportunity, fired upon him from ambush. Though severely wounded, he was able to get into the house and bar the door. The Indians then pulled out the chinking and shot between the logs. The family was defenseless.[2] James Thompson and his wife Elizabeth were killed; Alice and her sister Elizabeth were kidnapped, along with their neighbor Mrs. Caffrey and her young son.

---

[1]. Recollections of Alice Elizabeth (Betty) Hill Newsom (1853-1933) written shortly before her death. The original document is in the Family Collections of Roy Newsom, Jr., 4400 Belmont Park Terrace # 154, Nashville, TN 37215.

[2]. John Trotwood Moore, *Tennessee, The Volunteer State*, (Nashville: The S.J. Clarke Publishing Co., 1923) p 206-207.

Chapter 1: A Family of Courage and Determination

Elizabeth soon was scalped on the trail because she could not keep up with the captors.[1]

Again, in her own words plus two Tennessee historians, Moore[2] and Matthews[3], Alice tells the story of her captivity[4]:

The Indians made straight for the Creek nation with Mrs. Caffrey, her little boy and me. In a few days some men met us on the path that leads from the Cherokees to the Creeks. They dared not ask us our names, nor offer us a horse to relieve our fatigue, just in case it might make our condition worse. When I dared to complain that I was tired of walking, my captor replied that he would get briars and scratch my thighs, and that would make me walk fast.

Mrs. Caffrey, her son and I were carried off to Kialigee, a Creek town on the Tallapoosa River. A man named John O'Riley, an Irish trader, and Sarah Fletcher, a white prisoner the Indians had brought in, lived in the village. Mr. O'Riley had offered to purchase us at his price of a Negro each for our ransom. The Indians refused, saying they did not bring prisoners there to let them go back to the Virginia people but had brought them to punish and make victuals and work for them. The Indians also told Mr. O'Riley that they did not think he had so great love for the Virginia people, adding that if he were not so great a friend of theirs they would knock him on the head for the proposal and requested him never to talk so to them about it any more. In May of 1792 a man named James Orr came through the village and Mr. O'Riley sent word back to the Cumberland that Mrs. Caffrey and I were alive and that we were put in the fields to work.

Mrs. Caffrey was so afraid of the Indians that she would do everything they said do but I would do just the opposite. I told them I would rather die than stay with them. I would chop up the corn and leave the weeds. In traveling along they would give us pots to carry they cooked in and I would knock them against the rocks and break them.

And the Indians tied us up three different times and piled wood around us to burn us alive. They would call the chief and squaws to see the performance. I would say 'burn me, I would rather die than

---

[1]. Recollections of John Davis quoted in *The South-Western Monthly*, (Nashville: Wales and Roberts, 1852), p 212.

[2]. John Trotwood Moore, *Tennessee, The Volunteer State*, (Nashville: The S.J. Clarke Publishing Co., 1923), p 207.

[3]. Thomas Edwin Matthews, *General James Robertson*, (Nashville: The Parthenon Press), p 118.

[4]. Recollections of Alice Elizabeth (Betty) Hill Newsom (1853-1933) written shortly before her death. The original document is in the Family Collections of Roy Newsom, Jr., 4400 Belmont Park Terrace # 154, Nashville, TN 37215.

to stay with you all.' The old Chief would say to the braves to turn us aloose.

After a while working in the fields I got so tired that I cried so much that they put me back in house to pound meal.

It is hard to say how long John O'Riley bargained with the Indians for my freedom there at the village of Kialigee. But eventually they agreed and he traded them 800 weight of dressed deer skins valued at $266. From that time I was shown every consideration, and made as comfortable as circumstances would permit. Finally, I was brought in to the American Agency at Rock Landing Georgia early in May, 1794, after a captivity of more than two years. I finally arrived back home in late October 1794.

Sketch by George Horton Jr., courtesy of Rosa King Horton

Thought to have been built by Edmund and Alice Collinsworth, this home spanned nearly two hundred years through pioneer and Civil War history. It stood in the northern part of the present-day Crossings commercial development.

James Collinsworth's boyhood home[1]

---

[1]. Christine Cole Marshall and Joy Marshall, *With Good Will and Affection For Antioch*, (Franklin, TN: Hillsboro Press, 2002), p 95. A photocopy of a faded photo in the Family Collections confirms this sketch to be the actual Collinsworth home which burned in the 1960s.

Chapter 2 - Growing up in Antioch

About a year after Alice returned from captivity, she and Edmund met and fell in love. On December 14, 1795, Edmund and Alice's brother, Robert Thompson, signed the marriage bond.[1] They lived in a house Edmund built near the village of Antioch, about 10 miles southeast of Nashville. The family cemetery is on present-day Mt. View Road. Their 640 acres of land had been deeded to Alice and her sister Elizabeth back in 1791, from the estate of John Thompson, Alice's brother, who was killed by Indians while working in his fields.

Edmund farmed and made shoes for a living. Their farm had plenty of horses, cattle, sheep, hogs and geese.[2] Nearby Mill Creek gave rich bottom land and water for livestock for early farms yet its floodwaters would damage churches and buildings and threaten economic development.[3]

Edmund and Alice's family started growing in 1798 when Susan Eliza was born. Elizabeth Catherine came along in 1800, James in 1802, Benjamin Franklin in 1803, Parmelia Ann in 1807, John Thompson in 1808 and George Washington about 1810.

The first school in Antioch, no doubt where the Collinsworth children attended, was held in an old brick church situated on a high hill overlooking the small village. The church which housed the school was founded near its present location in 1810 and was the forerunner of the present Antioch Baptist Church. Its pastor, the Reverend William T. Derrick, was principal of the school. Although it was a pay school, enrollment was good.[4]

Quiet farm life did not last long for the aging Edmund. He was over fifty years of age when war with the Creek Indians broke out in 1812. He must have remembered vividly what Alice had suffered as a captive of the Creeks. Was it revenge for the havoc they caused Alice and her family or just his sense of duty to answer the call for volunteers again as he had done in the Revolutionary War?

Whatever the case, on December 20, 1813 he enlisted in the First Regiment of West Tennessee Mounted Volunteers, commanded by Col. N. T. Perkins, and served in the company of Capt. Matthew Patterson.[5] This regiment comprised the sixty-day volunteers enlisted to fill the depleted

---

[1]. Davidson Co. TN Clerk's Office at the Court House in Nashville, Tennessee.
[2]. Davidson Co. TN Will Book 7, p 5.
[3]. Christine Cole Marshall and Joy Marshall, *With Good Will and Affection For Antioch*, (Franklin, TN: Hillsboro Press, 2002), p ix.
[4]. Christine Cole Marshall and Joy Marshall, *With Good Will and Affection For Antioch*, (Franklin, TN: Hillsboro Press, 2002), p 37.
[5]. Byron and Samuel Sistler, *Tennesseans in the War of 1812*, (Nashville: Byron Sistler & Associates, 1992), p 134.

ranks of Gen. Andrew Jackson's rapidly dwindling army after the first campaign of the Creek War. Although the enlistment terms were short, this regiment saw some of the fiercest action of the Creek War at Emuckfau and Enotochopco where Jackson's army was nearly routed by attacking Creeks.[1]

Edmund was wounded in the battle of Emuckfau and when his term was over, he was mustered out on February 8, 1814 at Fayetteville, Tennessee, about 75 miles south of Antioch. After recovering for eight months, when Jackson's next call came, Edmund re-enlisted on September 8, 1814, serving in the First Regiment of Colonel Robert Dyer, in the Tennessee Mounted Volunteer Gunmen under Capt. Thomas Jones. He mustered in at Fayetteville and passed through Fort Hampton in north Alabama, to Baton Rouge, and finally to New Orleans.[2]

This regiment was part of General Coffee's Brigade that took part in the Battle of New Orleans, one of America's most dramatic battles and helped define the character of the young United States. It was a humiliating defeat for 8,000 invading British regulars and solidified American independence. Edmund Collinsworth not only served under the first president of the United States, General George Washington at Valley Forge in the winter of 1777, but also fought under General Andrew Jackson, the future president, at New Orleans. He concluded his term of enlistment and received his final discharge after 231 days on April 27, 1815, receiving five days additional pay and travel expenses.[3]

Less than a year later Edmund died, according to a family legend, as a result of cutting himself while whittling. Alice was left with a farm to tend and seven children to raise: Susan Eliza age 18, Elizabeth Catherine age 16, James age 14, Benjamin Franklin age 13, Parmelia Ann age 9, John Thompson age 7 and George Washington age 6.

---

[1]. Tennessee State Library and Archives, http://tn.gov/tsla/history/military/tn1812.htm Accessed 3/2/2011

[2]. Byron and Samuel Sistler, *Tennesseans in the War of 1812*, (Nashville: Byron Sistler & Associates, 1992), p 134.

[3]. Byron and Samuel Sistler, *Tennesseans in the War of 1812*, (Nashville: Byron Sistler & Associates, 1992), p 134.

Children of Edmund and Alice Thompson Collinsworth[1]

With frequent help from her brother, Robert, Alice raised her children in Antioch.

The first to leave home, Elizabeth, married Aristarcus Collins on December 15, 1821. Elizabeth and Stark, as he was called, would live a simple life and raise their five boys and two girls while farming in Antioch.

Susan Eliza married Mark Cockrill, the son of her father's half-brother on May 23, 1822. Quite unlike her sister, life with her husband would be filled with excitement and wealth.

Scorned by his elders, the young Mark sold the land inherited from his father to buy and breed Merino sheep. He bought his first flock in Washington D.C. and drove the dozen or so sheep on foot to Nashville. Mark's crowning achievement occurred at the 1851 Crystal Palace Exposition in London. Samples from his Merino sheep were awarded first prize for the finest wool in the world. Queen Victoria presented Mark with a gold medal. His sheep also earned him awards in Vienna, Paris, and Lexington, Kentucky, where he beat out Henry Clay's prized sheep. The silver cup awarded him on this occasion bore the inscription "Clay's Defeat."[2]

He established a vast farm of 5,600 acres called "Stock Place" six miles from Nashville on Charlotte Pike. At different times he also owned a cotton plantation in Mississippi and a plantation near Lexington, Kentucky. In 1854 he bought an additional 1,000 acres near Nashville, the famed Tulip Grove estate adjacent to the Hermitage, from Andrew Jackson Donelson for over fifty-three thousand dollars.[3]

His worth on the eve of the Civil War was estimated at two million dollars, making him one of the richest men in the state. The Civil War considerably diminished Cockrill's wealth, though, since the Union army confiscated much of his property, including hundreds of blooded livestock, twenty thousand bushels of corn, two hundred tons of hay, two thousand bushels of oats, and two thousand pounds of bacon. An unrepentant secessionist, Cockrill admitted to lending the Confederacy twenty-five thousand dollars in gold.[4]

---

[1]. **The children of Edmund Collinsworth and Alice Thompson Collinsworth:**

Full Name	Birth dates	Birth date source confirming family records
Susan Eliza	1/14/1798	1860 census Davidson Co. TN
Elizabeth Catherine	1800	1860 census Davidson Co. TN
James	1802	Apr 1823 Davidson Co. court minutes "has attained age 21"
Benjamin Franklin	2/22/1803	1850 census Gibson Co. TN
Parmelia Ann	1807	1860 census Davidson Co.TN
John Thompson	12/1808	U.S. Military Acad. "admitted 9/1/1826, age 17yr 9mo"
George Washington	1810	New Orleans ship passenger list 1831 "merchant, age 21"

[2]. http://tennesseeencyclopedia.net/entry.php?rec=285 Accessed 3/2/2011
[3]. http://tennesseeencyclopedia.net/entry.php?rec=285 Accessed 3/2/2011
[4]. http://tennesseeencyclopedia.net/entry.php?rec=285 Accessed 3/2/2011

Next to be married was Parmelia Ann, who married Loyd Davis May 28, 1823. After their marriage they began to live with her mother at the home place during the last few years of Alice's life. Like her sister Elizabeth, Parmelia raised her family near Antioch, thirty–plus years as a widow. She would remain in contact with her three unmarried brothers.

In 1823 Benjamin Franklin married Elizabeth Brownlee Mason and moved to Gibson Co. TN where they bought land from her father, Abram Mason, and raised many children there.

That left three boys, James possibly for another year or two, John and George still living at the home place, waiting for their time to come.

Chapter 3 – Antagonists and Friends

A Young Attorney in Nashville, 1823-1829

John Bell, a neighbor five or six years older than James, grew up on a farm less than a mile away from the Collinsworth family in Antioch. He graduated from Cumberland College in 1814, studied law and was admitted to the bar in 1816 and commenced practice in Franklin, TN. Entering politics, he successfully ran for the Tennessee State Senate in 1817 at age 21. After serving a single term, Bell declined to run for re-election and instead moved to Nashville. Surely, it was he who inspired James to follow in his footsteps as a lawyer and politician. Later, they would become partners in a law practice in Nashville, each preparing for greater challenges ahead.

Some well-known writers of Texas history (Kemp, Dixon, et al) assert that James Collinsworth began his law career in Columbia, Maury County, Tennessee in 1826 without giving the source for that location and date. James Collinsworth's name does not appear as being admitted to practice law in Maury County in the index of Maury County Court Minutes between August 1816 and August 1828 or in Chancery Court Minutes for a similar period.

James began his life in law in October of 1823 in Nashville, Davidson County, Tennessee. Minutes of the April 1823 session of the Davidson County Court record James' first step in becoming an attorney:

> *On motion of Lindsey C. Hall[1] esquire, and it appearing to the satisfaction of the court here that James Collinsworth is a man of good moral character and that he <u>hath attained the age of twenty one years</u>, it is ordered that he have a certificate hereof granted to him as a preparatory step to his obtaining license to practice law in this state.*[2]

About six months later, "James Collinsworth, Esquire came into court on October 21, 1823 and took the several oaths requisite to his qualification as an attorney at law and is admitted to practice law in this state."[3]

---

[1]. Lindsey C. Hall, Esq. was born about 1790 in Virginia and practiced law in Nashville until late 1825. He removed to Mississippi and became a Representative in the Mississippi Legislature from Yazoo Co. in 1826. He died about 1835 in Carroll Co. MS. [Robert Lowry and William H. McCardle, *History of Mississippi*, (Jackson MS, R. H. Henry & Co.1891, p 615)]

[2]. Davidson Co. TN County Court Minutes, April Sessions 1823, p 524.

[3]. Davidson Co. TN County Court Minutes, October Sessions 1823, p 598.

Admission to the Bar in Tennessee[1]

The license required by law from the date of the county's formation (in fact only from 1789) was to be issued by the state of North Carolina. In order to obtain a license, a candidate was required to be examined by two Superior Court judges, whose duty it was to ascertain "a competent Share of Law Knowledge" and an "upright Character" in the potential lawyer. No educational requirement was listed. Most Davidson County prospects for licensure had little and often nothing in the way of formal education. The legal training needed was usually obtained through "reading the law" under the guidance of a practicing attorney. Included in the ranks of those receiving their education this way were such influentials as John Overton and Andrew Jackson.

Prior to the 1834 Constitution, and to some extent afterwards, the General Assembly exercised considerable control over licensing procedures in the legal profession. The legislature in 1798 passed its first act specifically dealing with the profession, calling for examination by any two Superior Court judges of all bar applicants and requiring the following oath: "I, _____, do swear that I will truely and honestly demean myself in the practice of an attorney to the best of my skills and abilities."

These admissions standards were augmented in 1809 when a certificate from the County Court Clerk showing "good moral character" and age exceeding twenty-one years was required of all applicants. For this certificate a fee of five dollars was assessed (to be credited to the general education fund). An express disavowal of any required length of time in legal training was also passed.

Practice of Law in Tennessee[2]

Of all the professions [in early Nashville] the law carried the greatest weight and opened the most doors. Yet here, too, standards remained loose to non-existent. It was not until 1824 that the Tennessee Supreme Court set a "course of study" for candidates and began to insist on "close examination in open court." Sam Houston took time out at the beginning of his adventurous career to study in Judge Trimble's office and "in a few months was admitted to the bar." The next year he was made district attorney for Davidson County, paralleling the career of his mentor, Andrew Jackson.

One young merchant, Thomas Fletcher, bankrupted by the panic of 1819, became a lawyer and indeed one of the most successful and least solemn of the breed. Fletcher, who in 1827 became United States Attorney for the District of West Tennessee, may have written "History of a Modern

---

[1]. Article by R. Kreis White, David C. Rutherford, Ed., *Bench and Bar, Nashville Davidson Co. TN*, 1981, p 76.

[2]. Anita Shafer Goodstein, *Nashville 1780-1860 From Frontier to City*, (Gainesville: University of Florida Press), p 24.

Chapter 3: Antagonists and Friends

Attorney," a series of letters in the <u>Whig</u>, which explained that the law was one way for a "busted" businessman, despite ignorance and inexperience, to recoup his fortune. "Get what you can" was the answer to the novice's question about the proper fee. Law, too, was a business. Lawyers discovered that elevation to the bench was less lucrative than practice and, like Felix Grundy, they gave up judges' positions— though not the title. It is a cliché that eloquence and quickness rather than learning and precedents marked the way to success for frontier lawyers. Loudness might have helped, too, if the descriptions of procedures or lack of them, in the county courts are to be believed.

When James Collinsworth began practicing law in Nashville in 1823, Sam Houston was District Attorney, single and living at the Nashville Inn as was James. Both were members of the sporting crowd in their off hours and placed closely together in the courtroom during the day. They became quite good friends. In fact the pit used for cock fighting was next door to the Nashville Inn and both men were regular patrons. The same could be said for the horse races at Clover Bottom and the saloons around Nashville. Later in 1823 Sam ran and was elected to Congress. When he was home in the district, Sam and James were seen together quite often.[1]

James represented his siblings in court when their father's land was divided among the heirs on December 22, 1824. Edmund had bought the 200 acre tract on Hurricane Creek from his brother-in-law, Robert Thompson, on June 6, 1804.[2]

On January 1, 1825 for the sum of $300 James deeded to Lloyd Davis, his sister Parmelia's husband, Lot No. 4, his inherited division of land from the estate of his father.[3] Five days later Lloyd and Parmelia sold Lots 3 and 4 to John Hill for $600.[4]

Legal and political pots were beginning to simmer during the first quarter of the 19th century in middle Tennessee. Sam Houston was admitted to the Bar in 1819; James K. Polk was admitted to the Bar in June 1820. On March 4, 1823 Andrew Jackson was elected to the U.S. Senate, Sam Houston was elected to the U.S. House and James K. Polk was elected to the Tennessee House of Representatives.

John Quincy Adams was elected in the 1824 Presidential race that was decided in the U. S. House of Representatives according to the process under the 12th Amendment. In this election, no candidate received a majority of the electoral votes. Andrew Jackson led with 99 votes, followed by John Quincy Adams with 84, William Harris Crawford with 41 and Henry Clay with 37. The House of Representatives had to choose the president from the

---

[1]. Kimbrough Dunlap, a descendant of Benjamin Franklin Collinsworth and an early Collinsworth researcher, in a letter to James B. Collinsworth, Jr. dated November 29, 2000.

[2]. Davidson Co. TN Deed Book F, p 178.

[3]. Davidson Co. TN Deed Book R, p 405.

[4]. Davidson Co. TN Deed Book V, pp 382-383.

top three candidates. So Henry Clay gave his support to Adams, who was elected by the House. As a "reward" Adams then named Clay his Secretary of State, a step that Jackson supporters labeled the "Corrupt Bargain." Jackson would steam about this election over the next four years.

The location of James' law office can be determined by an April 30, 1825 note for office rent that was included in the additional inventory of the estate of John Baird,[1] who had owned adjacent town lots 38 and 50 on Cedar Street, facing the Davidson County court house.

Shortly after Houston was re-elected in 1825, he was appointed by Congress as the Chairman of the Congressional Board of Visitors of the U.S. Military Academy at West Point. I don't know what he did in that assignment with such a long title, but I do know it meant he had important West Point connections that led to the appointment of James' younger brother, John, to the United States Military Academy at West Point.[2] The seventeen-year-old John T. Collinsworth became a cadet on September 1, 1826, having been nominated by both Andrew Jackson Donelson and Sam Houston.[3]

On August 2, 1827, Sam Houston was elected Governor of Tennessee.

An Affair of Honor[4]

In September of 1827 a dramatic challenge faced the 25 year-old James Collinsworth. Here's how it happened:

James' friend, Willis Alston[5] was in Nashville as was David M. Saunders, an attorney and politician from Gallatin, Tennessee. Saunders was a step-brother of Andrew Jackson Donelson, the son of Rachel Donelson Jackson's brother, Samuel. David Saunders took offense to some remarks made by Willis Alston and the story, according to Saunders, unfolds in his own words written in letters to their mutual classmate at the University of North Carolina, William A. Graham:

... I was attacked in the public square in this place [Nashville] by Willis Alston formerly a member of our class to know whether or not

---

[1]. Helen C. and Timothy R. Marsh, Davidson Co. *Tennessee Wills and Inventories, Abstracts, Volume Two, 1716-1821*, (Greenville SC: 1990), p 190.

[2]. Kimbrough Dunlap, a descendant of Benjamin Franklin Collinsworth and an early Collinsworth researcher, in a letter to James B. Collinsworth, Jr. dated November 29, 2000.

[3]. *Register of the Officers and Cadets of the U.S. Military Academy, June 1830*.

[4]. J. G. de Roulhac Hamilton, Editor, *The Papers of William Alexander Graham, Vol. 1*, (Raleigh: State Department of Archives and History, 1957), pp 160-164.

[5]. Willis Alston (1803-1840) was a Georgian with roots in a military family in Hillsborough, North Carolina.

Chapter 3: Antagonists and Friends

I had ever used expressions calculated to injure him. He presented himself with his hand on a pistol for the purpose of alarming me, and to force me into an unqualified denial of the remarks I had made. It seems that about two months since while in Nashville I had in an incidental conversation observed that Mr. Alston was a gambler, and for using that expressing [sic] he alleged that I had slandered him.

A few days later I went to Nashville for the purpose of coming to more deffinate [sic] understanding with Mr. Alston, and after remaining several days I ascertained that Mr. Alston after having treated me in the most unauthorized and ungentlemanly manner and after having bound himself to assume the authorship of the report if no responsible author could be found, and after having circulated reports altogether unfounded, I addressed him a note admitting what he accused me of saying for the purpose of eliciting from him a challenge. This he avoided by a publication in which he used the epithets of coward, scoundrel and liar in reference to myself. I met his publication and satisfied the Citizens of Nashville that from the course he had pursued and the manner he had acted that he was no longer worthy to be noticed as a gentleman.

Shortly after my publication made its appearance he by the assistance of some one or two made another publication, and immediately after its appearance he made his exit for Georgia for the purpose—he alledged [sic]—of bringing his Brother to fight me.

Previous to his departure and after I had satisfied my friends and the public that he was unworthy of my notice, I challenged his friend and advisor [James Collinsworth].

Arrangements for the duel were made by a series of notes passed through their respective seconds:

Nashville, Sept. 19th,
Wednesday Evening,

Mr. James Collinsworth

Sir,
I have satisfactory evidence to convince me that you are acting as the aider, abetter & assistor of Willis Alston by exciting and encouraging him in his attempts to ruin my character. He sir, as I have satisfactorily proven to the world, is a man unworthy of notice. But you sir can be recognized in the light of a gentleman, though by identifying yourself with him, you are equally deserving of contempt. I call on you, sir, to unmask yourself and render me that satisfaction which one gentleman is bound to render another.
Yours etc.,
David M. Saunders

Nashville, Sept. 20th.
Thursday Evening.

Sir your impertinent note of yesterday was handed me by Capt. Peyton. Your wishes can be gratified, let me know what you want.
      Yours &c.
      James Collinsworth.

Nashville Sept. 20th
Thursday Evening.

James Collinsworth, Esqr.,
Sir, Your note of this date has been received by the hands of Mr. Washington, in which you pretend not to understand the exact import of a note sent you on yesterday. I will explain it. You have been instrumental in attempting to do me an injury. I therefore demand of you satisfaction in the manner that is resorted to by gentlemen.
      Yours etc.,
      D. M. Saunders.

Nashville, Thursday Evening,
Sept 20th.

Sir. Your note of this evening has been handed me by Capt. Peyton & I am willing to give you the satisfaction you require. My friend Mr. Washington is authorized to make arrangements for that purpose.
      Yours etc.,
      Jas. Collinsworth.

"The following are the stipulations by which we fought: In the affair of honour now pending between David M. Saunders & James Collinsworth, we, the friends, agree to meet on the 21st. of Sept. at 5 o'clock P. M. [1827] one half mile below David McGavock's ferry on the south side of Cumberland River… [and] that the arms should be rifles, and distance forty yards."

> Stip. 1st. The arms to be used by the parties are doubled triggered rifles, not to exceed three feet 10 inches in the barrels.
> Stip. 2nd. The principles to stand back to back 40 yards apart, with their heels to a line, their rifles to an order, triggers sprung but not cocked.
> Stip. 3rd. The friends of the parties shall throw up for the word, and the gentlemen winning the word shall repeat it an audible distinct voice, three times before the parties take their stands, so that each principal may understand the manner of giving it, & it

shall be repeated in the same manner and tone of voice while the parties take their stands as he did before.

Stip. 4th. The manner of giving the word shall be make ready—fire. And neither party shall change his position, or move his gun from an order until the word fire is given.

Stip. 5th. Each principal shall load his own gun with one smooth round leaden ball, in the presence of the friends of both parties.

Stip. 6th. The principals to be in their shirts and pantaloons, and each principal to be examined by the friend of his antagonist, to see that there is nothing about his person to impede the progress of the ball.

Stip. 7th. If either party change his position, or move his gun, he shall be shot down by the friend of the other party.

Stip. 8th. After the word fire is given the parties shall be allowed six seconds to each and fire.

Stip. 9th. There shall be a person selected by each party to keep the time, who shall at the expiration of six seconds cry halt. If either party fire after the word halt, he is to be shot down by the friend of the other party.

Stip. 10th. A snap or a flash is to be considered a fire.

Stip. 11th. The seconds shall stand half way between the parties face to face, each having a loaded pistol.

Stip. 12th. We are under a pledge of honor that no person shall be present or in sight, with our consent, except the time keepers.

Stip. 13th. The parties when firing shall stand erect—there shall be no stooping.

Stip. 14th. We pledge our honours [sic] that every stipulation in this article shall be faithfully adhered to, under the penalty that the party violating any of them shall be shot down. Sept. 20th, 1827."   *Balie Peyton*[1]
         Wm. Washington[2].

"These stipulations were presented about half after 10 o'clock on Thursday night and signed by the seconds on the next morning and the meeting took place about 5 o'clock of the evening of the same day."

"We accordingly met about two miles and a half below Nashville and fought agreeably to the stipulations. My Antagonist, James Collinsworth, Esq., was shot throu [sic] his left hand, the ball cutting

---

[1]. Balie Peyton (1803-1878), a native of Tennessee, lawyer, Whig member of congress, 1833-1837; moved to Louisiana in 1841, and served as federal district attorney, on staff duty in the Mexican War, minister to Chile, 1849-1853; lived in California, 1853-1859, and then returned to Tennessee, where he was a Bell and Everett elector, 1860, and state senator, 1869-1870. [*Biographical Directory of the United States Congress*]

[2]. William Washington was an attorney with a law practice in Nashville.

the two fore fingers of the right hand, glancing from his gun and striking him on his chinn [sic], then in his shoulder a little above his niple [sic] and has there lodged, and I have since understood that it cannot be extracted. I received merely a slight tuch [sic] on my right rist [sic] without doing me any injury."

"I had made preperation [sic] to start to N. Carolina but have learned that my Antagonist will unquestionably recover. This is for you and the rest of my Hillsboro friends. In speaking of this matter I do not wish you to give any one to understand except a few of my friends that I have written to you on the subject. It is too delicate a matter for me to talk or wright [sic] about. There was a desperate effort made to ruin me and my character. I have met them on their own ground, and have maintained my honour [sic] and my character."

After surviving the harrowing experience of a duel and the pompous remarks of his antagonist, life goes on for James. On January 15, 1828 he signed a promissory note to Joseph Nash in the amount of $83.97.

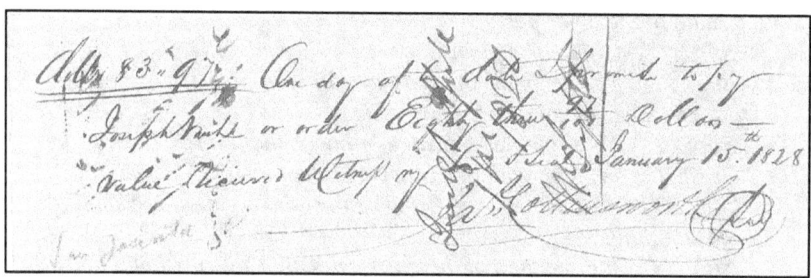

James' mother, Alice Thompson Collinsworth, died in the early months of 1828, bringing to a close one of the most remarkable stories of survival in the over-mountain frontier. From Antrim to Antioch, she met life's challenges and left to her children a legacy of determination and character. On March 18, 1828 the sale of the estate of Alice Collinsworth was recorded by her son and administrator.[1]

The Presidential Election of 1828[2]

The Election of 1824 left supporters of Andrew Jackson bitterly disappointed. He had garnered the most electoral votes, but had been denied the presidency by the House of Representatives.

---

[1]. Helen C. and Timothy R. Marsh, *Davidson Co. Tennessee Wills and Inventories, Abstracts, Volume Two, 1716-1821*, (Greenville SC: 1990), p 200.

[2]. http://www.u-s-history.com/pages/h325.html Accessed 3/4/2011

The Election of 1828 was unique in that nominations were no longer made by Congressional caucuses, but by conventions and the state legislatures. John Quincy Adams was re-nominated by forces then calling themselves the National Republicans; his running mate was Secretary of the Treasury Richard Rush. The Democratic Republican (soon to be simply Democratic) opposition was posed by Jackson and his vice-presidential candidate, John C. Calhoun, who had previously been vice president under Adams.

The campaign was a true mud-slinging contest. Adams was accused of misusing public funds — he had supposedly purchased gambling devices for the presidential residence; actually he had simply bought a chessboard and a pool table. The charges against Jackson were much more malicious. He was accused of murder for executing militia deserters and for dueling. In addition, he and his wife were accused of adultery. Rachel was a divorcee'; she and Jackson believed her divorce was finalized before their marriage. The papers were incomplete, however, and she was branded an adulteress by Jackson's political opponents. Mrs. Jackson was humiliated, became ill and died before the inauguration. Jackson believed these attacks caused his wife's death and said, "May God Almighty forgive her murderers as I know she forgave them. I never can."

The election results were a clear victory for Jackson, but were highly sectional in nature. The South, West, and the states of Pennsylvania and New York went for Jackson; New England voted for Adams. The final tally of popular vote showed Jackson with 647,286 votes against 508,064 for Adams.

An Inaugural Ball celebrating Andrew Jackson's election to the presidency was planned for December, 1828 but did not occur due to the untimely death of Rachel, his wife. James was one of the managers coordinating the ball.

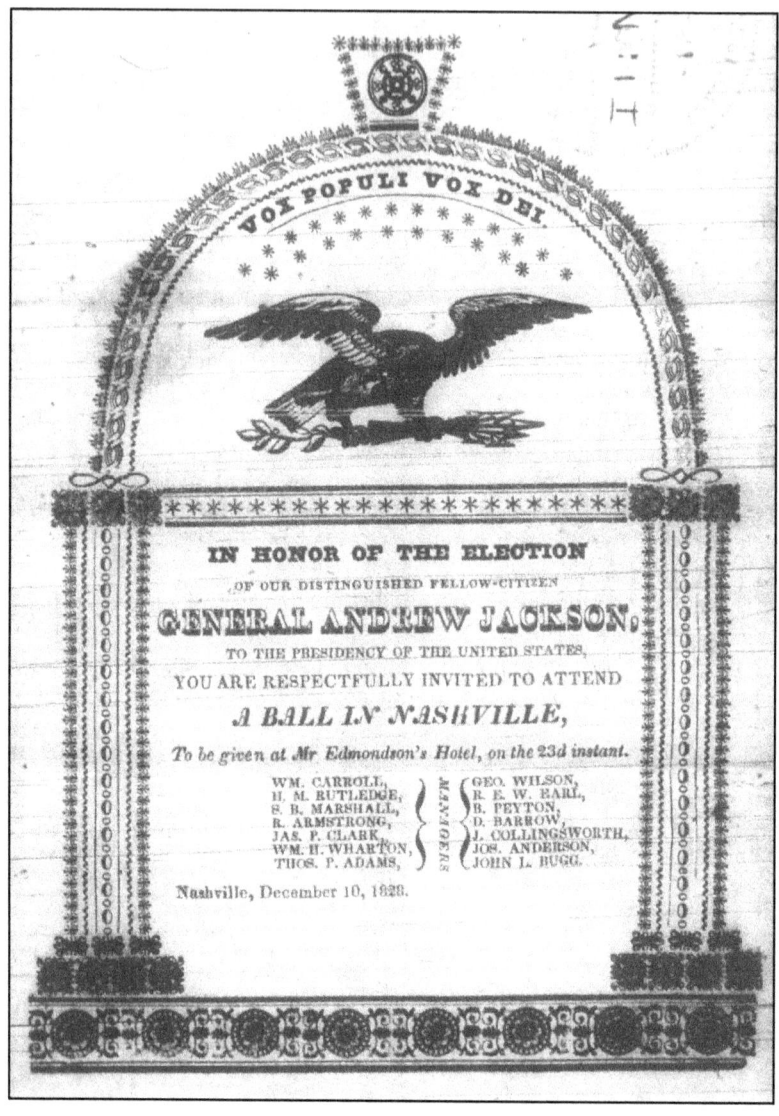

Invitation to the Inaugural Ball, December 10, 1828 in Nashville[1]

---

[1]. Tennessee State Library and Archives, Tennessee Historical Society Miscellaneous Files, Mf. 678, Reel 4, Box 7, I-12

Chapter 4 – The President Appoints an Attorney

United States Attorney for the District of West Tennessee, 1829-1835

The source of letters in this chapter regarding the office of United States Attorney for the District of West Tennessee[1], except as noted, are recorded in President Andrew Jackson's papers as transcribed[2] and also as microfilm copies of the original documents.[3]

On March 4, 1829 Andrew Jackson became President of the United States. Shortly after his inauguration, Thomas Fletcher[4], United States Attorney for the District of West Tennessee sent his letter of resignation:

Nashville April 7 1829

Sir,
 I hereby resign the office of Attorney of the United States for the District of West Tennessee.
 And although I am sure the President can feel no concern about the motive which induces me to take this step, yet, as an act of justice to myself I beg leave to say that I am not impelled by any feeling of hostility towards General Jackson either personally or politically. On the contrary, as his forbearance down to this time has manifested a disposition to retain me in office, I cannot but feel gratitude for his kindness.
           With respect and esteem I remain
           Your ob't svt

           Thos. H. Fletcher

But the word was already out that Fletcher intended to resign as United States Attorney for the District of West Tennessee – nineteen letters of application or recommendations were penned before the date of Fletcher's resignation.

---

[1]. The area called West Tennessee in this chapter refers to present-day Middle Tennessee.
[2]. Harold D. Moser, David R. Hoth, and George H. Hoemann, Editors, *The Papers of Andrew Jackson 1829, Vol. VII*, (Knoxville: The University of Tennessee Press), pp 702-715.
[3]. Tennessee State Library and Archives Record Group 59 and Atlanta Regional National Archives Series M639-5.
[4]. Thomas H. Fletcher would later hold the office of Secretary of State of Tennessee, 1830-1832.

The first among the applications was from James Collinsworth to William B. Lewis[1] asking Lewis to forward his application letter to the appropriate party:

Nashville
4th April 1829

Dear Sir,

Mr. Fletcher having determined to resign his office of District Atty I would be glad [if] you would as far as you do not feel yourself restrained by a sense of propriety represent my claim to the proper department as an applicant for that office in such way as you think I may deserve. With sentiments of respect I am your friend and ob't servant.

Jas. Collinsworth

William B. Lewis Esqr.

---

[1]. William Berkeley Lewis (1784 - November 12, 1866) was born in Loudoun County, Virginia, and later moved near Nashville, Tennessee, in 1809. Major Lewis served as quartermaster under General Andrew Jackson. Later, in politics, he was a manager of Jackson and retained considerable influence until Jackson's second term as President of the United States. Jackson appointed Lewis as second auditor of the Treasury, a position he was able to retain until the Polk administration. [Ratner, Lorman. *Andrew Jackson and His Tennessee Lieutenants: A Study in Political Culture*, 1997]

Chapter 4: The President Appoints an Attorney

The second letter was from James to President Andrew Jackson himself:

Nashville
4th April 1829

Dear Sir
Mr. Thomas H. Fletcher having announced his intention of resigning his office as district Atty on Sunday past I would respectfully submit my qualifications as an applicant for that office & will as soon as practicable forward some testimonials of qualification.

Respectfully your ob't Servant
Jas. Collinsworth

His Excellency A. Jackson
President of the U. States

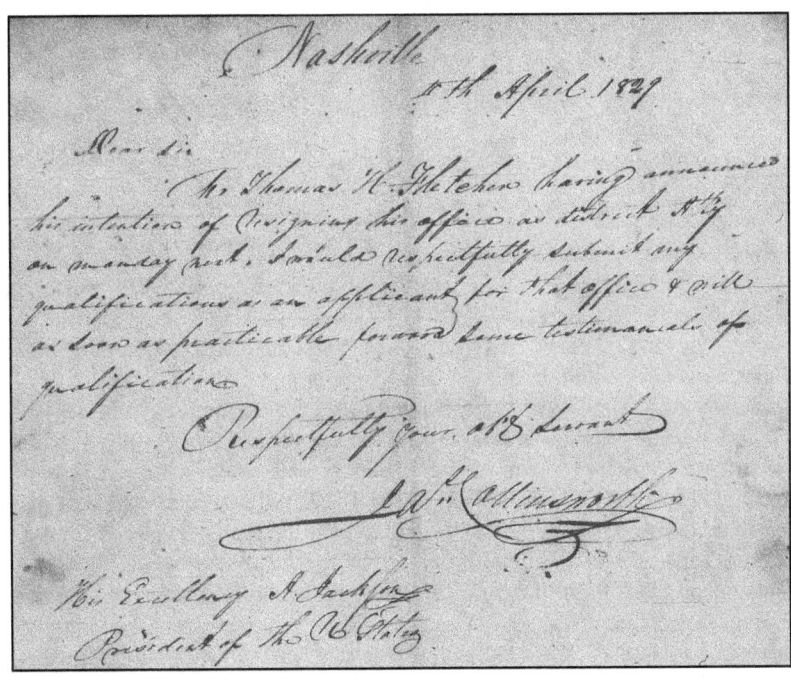

James' strategy in seeking the office of United States Attorney for the District of West Tennessee was to solicit recommendations from his friends and law associates who also were confidants of President Jackson, knowing

their letters of recommendation would strongly influence the president's decision. Transcribed here are five letters of recommendation:
Ephraim Hubbard Foster[1] sent this recommendation on James' behalf:

> Martin Van Buren *Esq.*
> Nashville, April 4th 1829
>
> Sir,
>   *The resignation of Thos. H. Fletcher having created a vacancy in the office of District Attorney in this District, I take the liberty to submit the name of James Collinsworth Esq as his successor.*
>   *Mr. Collinsworth is a gentleman of fine talents and with a character unimpeachable in every respect. He possesses habits of industry and attention, which added to his very superior legal qualifications will, I am sure, secure to the government an <u>able, efficient</u> & <u>faithful</u> officer.*
>
>   *I am*
>   *Most respectfully*
>   *Your ob't Servant*
>   *Ephraim H. Foster*

---

[1]. Ephraim Hubbard Foster, a Senator from Tennessee; born near Bardstown, Nelson County, Ky., September 17, 1794; moved to Tennessee with his parents, who settled near Nashville, Davidson County, in 1797; completed preparatory studies and graduated from Cumberland College (later the University of Nashville) in 1813; studied law; admitted to the bar in 1820 and commenced practice in Nashville, Tenn.; served in the Creek War and was private secretary to Gen. Andrew Jackson 1813-1815; member, State house of representatives 1829-1831, 1835-1837, and served as speaker during that time; appointed as a Whig to the United States Senate to fill the vacancy caused by the resignation of Felix Grundy, and served from September 17, 1838, to March 3, 1839; was reelected for the term beginning March 4, 1839, but resigned, not wishing to obey instructions given him by the State legislature; chairman, Committee on Claims (Twenty-eighth Congress); elected to the United States Senate to fill the vacancy caused by the death of his successor, Felix Grundy, and served from October 17, 1843, to March 3, 1845; unsuccessful Whig candidate for Governor in 1845; resumed the practice of law; died in Nashville, Tenn., September 6, 1854; interment in the City Cemetery.
[http://bioguide.congress.gov/scripts/biodisplay.pl?index=f000302 Accessed 10/17/2012]

Chapter 4: The President Appoints an Attorney

This recommendation came from Thomas Crutcher[1]:
Nashville Inn Tennessee
4th of April 1829

Dear Sir
Mr. James Collinsworth has made application to me to say to you what I may think of him as an Attorney for the United States. I am not a sufficient judge to say anything about Mr. Collinsworth's qualifications as an attorney. As the same kind of request was made by Mr. Barrow's friends, I can only say that Mr. Collinsworth I believe to be a sober moral young man and bears the character of an honest young man. Both _____ Eaton and Lewis are acquainted with Mr. Collinsworth.

Respectfully
Your ob't Servant
Tho. Crutcher

Because of close family relationships this recommendation from David Craighead that must have carried significant weight with the President:[2]

Jones Bend April 5 1829

Dear Sir
Thos. Fletcher attorney of the US for this district intends to resign that appointment. Several young gentlemen will be applicants for the office. Amongst them Mr. James Collingsworth.
It must be perplexing to select amongst a number of young gentlemen who are all amicable, patriotic, capable, and not entirely out of the reach of want. All that I have heard mentioned as being likely to offer are of that description. I hope I do no injustice to any by saying that in my opinion Mr. Collingsworth is one of the most

---

[1]. Thomas Crutcher born in 1760 in Virginia. He was elected and served as mayor of Nashville, Tennessee in 1819-20. He was a Trustee of the Branch Bank of the State of Tennessee. He was buried in the Nashville City Cemetery in 1844.

[2]. David Craighead, the second son of Rev. Thomas and Elizabeth Brown Craighead, was born in the year 1790, and married in 1820 Mrs. Mary Hunt Goodloe, formerly Macon, daughter of John Macon, of Warrenton, N. C, and grand-niece of Hon. Nathaniel Macon. She died in Nashville in 1872, greatly beloved and respected. Mr. Craighead was a lawyer of distinction in Nashville, Tenn., a man of superior talents, and a public speaker in great repute. Although he was educated as a lawyer he seldom practiced. He was a member of the state senate 1835-37. Some years previous to his death, which took place in Memphis, January, 1849, he removed to Arkansas, and largely engaged in operations as a planter. [*The Craighead family* By James Geddes Craighead]

promising young gentlemen in our profession. And I am satisfied such is the opinion of the public. And I will take upon myself to affirm that if appointed he will fill the office with fidelity and talents.

Your farm is in most excellent order _____ will I think satisfy our expectations. I rode all around and over your farm and my friend Donalson's [page2] very lately. If any further improvement could be made or desired I could not discover it.

In recommending Mr. Collingsworth I _____ express my candid belief that he will be an excellent appointment and very acceptable to the people. As to _____ing you dear sir with my individual wishes or partiality that is wholly out of the question. I have not forgotten nor has any who bear my name that we are already your debtor to a boundless extent.

For twenty five years has his church[1] denied to our venerable father the _____ right of a public and fair trial condemning him absent and unheard no (entreaty) no _____ no _____ of his few clerical friends could gain him a moments attention. The

---

[1]. In the first decade of the 19th century, Thomas Craighead, David's father, had fallen under the displeasure of his Synod, and a commission it had appointed, propounded to Mr. Craighead a series of questions, thirty-one in number, designed to test his belief in the doctrines of the Church.

The Presbytery of Transylvania summoned Mr. Craighead to appear before it in April, and again in October, 1810. He could not attend either meeting, and at the latter was suspended. This decision was approved by the Synod of Kentucky, and Mr. Craighead appealed to the General Assembly, the court of last resort. The controversy continued—it may easily be imagined with how much bitterness—until 1824, when it finally came for trial before the Assembly. This Presbytery, in 1824, satisfied with Mr. Craighead's statements, reinstated him in the ministry.

This particular controversy had lasted nearly fifteen years, but Mr. Craighead's differences with his church covered a much longer period. The quietus was finally given to the prosecution by General Jackson, who declared the matter had gone too far, and was injuring not only Mr. Craighead, but the church.

It seems certain that Jackson was the staunch friend of Mr. Craighead, and there were many reasons for it. Their residences, though separated by the Cumberland River, were but a few miles apart; they were associated as trustees of the academy and the college; both belonged to the same church and were descendants of Scotch-Irish immigrants. Jackson's mother is said to have found shelter -with members of Alexander Craighead's congregation in North Carolina when she followed her son to Charleston, whither he had been carried a prisoner by the British, and was, during her last illness, cared for by a sister of Thomas Craighead. [A V Goodpasture, Editor, *American Historical Magazine and Tennessee Historical Society Quarterly, Vol. VII* (Nashville: Goodpasture Book Co., 1902), pp 88-96]

Chapter 4: The President Appoints an Attorney

church was too much occupied with the _____ _____ ___ until you in the midst of your own pressing engagements stepped forward and obtained for him that acquittal which justice had so long in vain demanded. You wiped the tear from his _____ eye and sent him in peace to his _____ grave. May the God he worshiped reward you [page 3] your kindness to his servant and give to the _____ of your life the serenity which you obtained for his dying pillow.
Very respectfully Yrs
David Craighead

This recommendation was sent by James Rucks[1]:

Lebanon 8th April 1829
Dear Sir
I am just informed that Thos. H. Fletcher Esq U S Atto at N[ashville] has or will shortly resign that appointment. I am not apprised that there will be any other applicant, but am authorized to say that Mr. Collinsworth would gladly accept it, and I have no doubt he would discharge the duties as ably & faithfully & give as much general satisfaction as any other individual who may apply.
We have general health & great tranquility. Accept my warmest wishes for your health and prosperity ---
James Rucks
Andrew Jackson, P. U. S

---

[1]. James Rucks was born in the county of Granville and State of North Carolina. His parents removed to the State of Tennessee when he was in his seventeenth year. He soon returned to the State of his nativity for the completion of his collegiate education. Having taken the customary degrees at the University of North Carolina, he returned to Tennessee, read law diligently and successfully for two years, and commenced the practice of his profession in Carthage, then a most promising town, where he soon obtained a profitable business, in competition with some of the ablest attorneys that Tennessee could then boast. He is reported by his friends of that period to have been singularly industrious in the preparation of his cases, and remarkably clear and forcible in his manner of discussing them in Court.

Rucks subsequently located in the town of Lebanon, where he remained until about the year 1828, when he removed to the city of Nashville, and was associated in business with the celebrated Felix Grundy, and General George Gibbs. He afterwards became one of the Circuit Judges of Tennessee, and, in that responsible position, gave universal satisfaction. [Henry S. Foote, *The Bench and Bar of the South and Southwest*, (St. Louis: Soule, Thomas & Wentworth, 1876), pp 90-91.]

Robert L. Cobbs[1] sent this recommendation:

Columbia April 28 1829

Dear General
   I am informed that T. H. Fletcher of Nashville has resigned his office as attorney of the United States for this District. I am also told that Mr. James Collinsworth of that place is a candidate for the office and have been requested to write you what I think of him. I have been acquainted with him about four years, believe him a gentleman a man of candor, independence and integrity, who will not disappoint any trust reposed in him.
   As to his qualifications, I have not so good an opportunity of judging: Yet I have seen pleadings that he has ____ ____ , briefs of his cases in courts, have heard him speak in some ____ cases, and have a tolerable knowledge of the _____ in which he is ____ by the more distinguished members of the bar that practice in the same

---

[1]. Robert Lewis Cobbs was born on December 25, 1789, in Virginia. He attended Hampden-Sydney College. Cobbs moved from Virginia to Tennessee in 1813. He resided in Columbia, Maury County, Tennessee where he practiced law.

   In the War of 1812 he was a surgeon for the 2nd Regiment of Tennessee Militia, General Coffee's Brigade: on March 3, 1815 he certified that Rose, a free girl of color, was entitled to be paid $10 for the month as washerwoman in the brigade hospital. Signatures: Robert L. Cobbs, SSCB; and David C. Ker, Hosp. Surg. USA. Endorsed by Maj. General Andrew Jackson; signature: Andrew Jackson, Major Gen. Comdg.

   In 1817 he was named by the State Legislature as Solicitor-general to the newly-formed Ninth District which included Giles, Maury, Lawrence, and Hickman Counties. He served in that position until 1825.

   In the year 1825, the Legislature of Tennessee passed an act providing, that there should be a Digest and Revision of the Statute Laws of this State, made in such manner, that when there were several statutes on the game subject, the whole might be reduced into one, in which should be comprehended the provisions contained in each, with marginal notes, shewing the date of the passage of the several acts, and stating the substance of each section. The *plan* of the work being thus prescribed to the late Judge Haywood and Robert L. Cobbs, Esq. was assigned the important task of performing it. Before the work was finished, Judge Haywood died—Mr. Cobbs completed it, and submitted it to the Legislature in 1827, ready for publication. He was directed to include the acts of that year, and to avail himself of the assistance of the late Wm. L. Brown, Esq., whenever it might be necessary, which he did. [William C. Cook Collection: The War of 1812 in the South, The Williams Research Center, The Historic New Orleans Collection and The Statute Laws of the State of Tennessee]

Chapter 4: The President Appoints an Attorney

courts with him. Upon the whole I consider him a man of natural and _____ above mediocrity, in a very respectable degree, one who possesses much of laudable ambition, study habits and industry as will ensure his best exertions in discharging the duties of the office.

His law knowledge is very respectable for one of his age at the bar, and I consider him as more distinguishable for accuracy of judgment and correctness of information than for an imposing manner of elocution, though highly respectable in this latter _____. I think he would fill the office well ____ ____. I expect you have information from Col. [John] Bell, of whom he is a partner, more satisfactory than I can give. I believe his appointment would be very acceptable to the Public.

I do not know that, according to the _____ forms of doing business. I am correct in ____ you personally on this subject _____. I ought to have addressed my letter to one of the departments. If so, my ignorance of _____ must be my _____, and also the gratification I feel in addressing yourself where you are.

> *With great respect your friend*
> *Robert L. Cobbs*

The office of United States Attorney for the District of West Tennessee was widely sought in 1829 among the attorneys practicing in Nashville. Below is a list of all the candidates and their recommenders:

Date	Candidate	Recommended by
4/4	James Collinsworth	self: forward application to appropriate party (to William B. Lewis)
4/4	James Collinsworth	self
4/4	James Collinsworth	Ephraim H. Foster
4/4	David Barrow	Andrew Hayes & Charles Jones Love
4/4	George M Dallas	J Johnston
4/4	Thomas A Duncan	Henry Alexander Wise
4/5	James Collinsworth	Thomas Crutcher
4/5	James Collinsworth	David Craighead
4/5	Archibald W Goodrich	self
4/5	William A Cook	asks A J Donelson to recommend him
4/6	David Barrow	Washington Barrow
4/6	Morgan W Brown	self
4/6	Morgan W Brown	William Little Brown
4/6	William A Cook	self
4/6	David Barrow	Nathan Ewing
4/6	Washington I Hannum	self
4/6	David Barrow	Robert Purdy
4/6	Morgan W Brown	Felix Robertson

4/6	David Barrow	Thomas A Duncan
4/7	James P Clark	William E Anderson
4/7	David Barrow	Samuel Hogg
4/8	David Barrow	William McLean Berryhill
4/8	Robert M. Burton	Samuel Hervey Laughlin
4/8	James Collinsworth	James Rucks
4/9	James P Clark	John Christmas McLemore
4/12	William A Cook	Frederick Watts Huling
4/13	William A Cook	John Hartwell Marable
4/15	John H Martin	self
4/16	William A Cook	William Claiborne Dunlap
4/20	William A Cook	Mortimer A Martin
4/21	William A Cook	Alexander M Clayton & Joseph Chilton
4/28	James Collinsworth	Robert L Cobbs

Andrew Jackson corresponded with Martin Van Buren regarding the appointing of James as successor to Thomas Fletcher as United States Attorney for the District of West Tennessee:

April 24th. 1829

Mr. Van Buren.

Respecting the appointment at Nashville (Attorney) I shall leave that to you; fair reciprocity is always right, and as I have given you, in your State, a Collector, I leave you, in mine, to give us an Attorney; asking nothing more than that you will give us as qualified a man. I have directed all the recommendations to be sent you for the applicants for this office. Yours &c

Andrew Jackson[1]

April 24 1829.

Dear Sir.

…… I shall cheerfully do what you may desire in regard to the appointment at Nashville but as I have not the slightest choice between the Candidates and no personal knowledge of either of them save Mr. Balch[2] *& that very superficially, I should be in no small degree embarrassed in the execution of a trust you have in so kind &C flattering a manner committed to me. But we shall converse on this subject further when I have the pleasure of seeing you.*

Your friend
M. Van Buren[3]

---

[1]. Printed, The Autobiography of Martin Van Buren, p. 265 (13-0136).
[2]. Alfred Balch (1785-1853) was a Nashville lawyer.
[3]. Copy (partly in Van Buren's hand), DLC-Van Buren Papers (13-0138).

Chapter 4: The President Appoints an Attorney

James was appointed United States Attorney for the District of West Tennessee by President Jackson on April 30, 1829 in this simple note to Martin Van Buren:

April 30 1829

To Martin Van Buren

I appoint James Collinsworth attorney for the District of west Tennessee ____, Thomas Fletcher resigned April 30th 1829.

Andrew Jackson

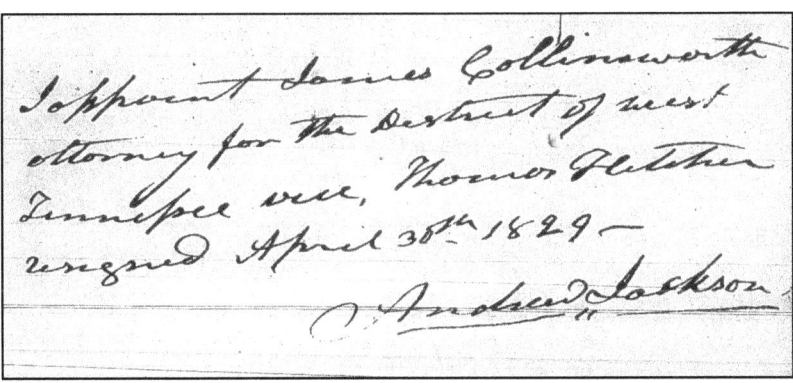

Apparently there was some surprise or concern among Jackson's cohorts that prompted Jackson to provide some further explanation through Felix Grundy:

Grundy to Jackson[1]

(private)

Nashville, May 22nd 1829

Dear Sir,

A few days since, I received [sic]your esteemed favor of the 2nd instant, and now proceed to answer—All are now satisfied with the appointment of Mr. Collinsworth as atto[sic] for this District—I conversed with Judge Brown & Mr. Clark[2] fully and freely on that subject—I also conversed with Gov. Carroll on the subject, named by you, he appeared much gratified at the fact of your noticing him in the way you did, and spoke very freely & in strong terms of commendation & friendship of you & your administration and at my

---

[1]. ALS, DLC (37). Grundy (1777-1840) was a Nashville lawyer and a former congressman.

[2]. William Little Brown (1789-1830), a former legislator and judge, and James P. Clark.

request furnished the inclosed [sic] answer to my inquiry—From it, you will discover, that it is inconsistent with his situation and views at present to accept of such appointment as is contemplated[1]—he I have no doubt entertains a hope, that at some future period, it will be found consistent with the public interest to provide for him, in a suitable manner—I hope so too—the military is certainly the place for him—and as he will be Governor of the State, things need not be hurried, events can be waited for—On the subject of the National Bank, you have in view—I admire the project and believe, that the president of the U States, who shall accomplish it, will have atcheived [sic] more for his Country, than has been effected by any act of Legislation, since the foundation of the Government—I will furnish as early as I can my views at large on that subject—agreeably to your request— [several paragraphs omitted]

I am sorry to inform you, that Malvina's father in law Mr. Peter Bass our old friend died at the mouth of Cumberland three days since—My family is well, and Mrs. Grundy unites with me in wishing you health & prosperity—yr friend
Felix Grundy

Although confirmation by the U. S. Senate would not be given until February, 1830, James' term as United States Attorney for the District of West Tennessee began on May 25, 1829[2].

---

[1]. Grundy enclosed a May 21 letter from Carroll (DLC-37) declining an appointment in light of his expected election as governor, but pledging AJ his "honest and faithful support."

[2]. Records of the District Court of the United States for the District of West Tennessee, p 442.

James' "first day at the office" was reported in a Richmond VA newspaper:
Nashville, June 10, [1829]. --- Hon. John McLean, Judge of the Supreme Court of the United States, arrived in this town on Saturday evening last, promptly to enter upon his official duties here; and yesterday the annual trial term of the U. States' Circuit Court for the District of West Tennessee, commenced at the City Hall - present Judges McLean and McNairy. James Collingsworth, Esq. our new District Attorney likewise entered upon the discharge of his public trust.[1]

Cases Prosecuted - May Term 1829
The Postmaster General of the United States vs Levi Holland[2]
Appearance bail for William Bloodworth.
Continued by consent.

The Postmaster General of the United States vs James Whiteside & Archibald Rhea[3]
Debt
Will no longer prosecute this suit. Dismissed.

The United States vs Stephen Cantrell, adm. for Howell Tatum dec'd[4]
Trespass
Will no longer prosecute this suit.
That the United States will recover against the defendant their costs.

John Gilbert vs The United States[5]
Habeas Corpus
Discharged from custody.

Cases Prosecuted - November Term 1829
The United States vs William Robertson and William [illegible][6]
Misdemeanor
Dismissed and United States pay costs.

---

[1]. Richmond Enquirer (Richmond Virginia), June 30, 1829.
[2]. Records of the District Court of the United States for the District of West Tennessee, p 442.
[3]. Records of the District Court of the United States for the District of West Tennessee, p 442.
[4]. Final Record Books of the U.S. District Court in Nashville 1806-1850, p 326.
[5]. Final Record Books of the U.S. District Court in Nashville 1806-1850, p 326.
[6]. Final Record Books of the U.S. District Court in Nashville 1806-1850, p 327.

James's formal notice of nomination[1] was sent to the U.S. Senate on January 5, 1830:
> James Collinsworth, of Tennessee, to be Attorney of the United States for the Western District of Tennessee, in place of Thomas Fletcher, resigned.
>
> Andrew Jackson

Formal advise and consent[2] passed by the U.S. Senate, February 16, 1830:
> Whereupon, Resolved, that the Senate advise and consent to the appointments of James Collinsworth and William A. Harrison.

James is listed as single head of household in the 1830 census of Davidson Co. TN. Also in 1830, boyhood friends John Bell and James Collinsworth formed a law partnership. On the front page of the National Banner and Nashville Whig of May 4, 1830 was the following legal announcement:
> John Bell[3] and James Collinsworth have formed a partnership in the practice of law. They will attend all the courts they have heretofore been in the habit of attending; their office is the one formerly occupied by J. Collinsworth.

---

[1]. *Journal of the Senate of the United States of America, 1789-1873, January 5, 1830*, p 398.

[2]. *Journal of the Senate of the United States of America, 1789-1873; Tuesday, February 16, 1830*, p 416.

[3]. John Bell, a Representative and a Senator from Tennessee; born near Nashville, Tenn., February 18, 1796; graduated from Cumberland College in 1814; studied law; admitted to the bar in 1816 and commenced practice in Franklin, Tenn.; member, State senate 1817; declined to be a candidate for reelection and moved to Nashville; elected to the Twentieth, and to the six succeeding Congresses (March 4, 1827-March 3, 1841); Speaker of the House of Representatives (Twenty-third Congress); chairman, Committee on Indian Affairs (Twenty-first through Twenty-sixth Congresses, except for Twenty-third), Committee on Judiciary (Twenty-second and Twenty-third Congresses); appointed by President William Henry Harrison as Secretary of War March 5, 1841, and served until September 12, 1841, when he resigned; member, State house of representatives in 1847; elected as a Whig to the United States Senate in 1847; reelected in 1853, and served from November 22, 1847, to March 3, 1859; unsuccessful candidate in 1860 for President of the United States on the Constitutional Union ticket; investor in ironworks at Cumberland Furnace, Tenn.; died at his home on the banks of the Cumberland River, near Cumberland Furnace, September 10, 1869; interment in Mount Olivet Cemetery, near Nashville, Tenn. [*Dictionary of American Biography*; Parks, Joseph H. *John Bell Of Tennessee*. Baton Rouge: Louisiana State University Press, 1950.]

Chapter 4: The President Appoints an Attorney

On July 1, 1830 James' brother, John Thompson Collinsworth, graduated from the U. S. Military Academy at West Point. He entered in the Army as a Second Lieut., Fifth Infantry, July 1, 1830. At the General Examination in June 1830 he was listed 24th in his class of 42.[1] He served on frontier duty at Ft. Mackinac, Michigan 1830-1831; Ft. Howard, Wisconsin, 1831-1832; Ft. Brady, Michigan, 1832-1833; and Ft. Winnebago, Wisconsin, 1833-1834.[2] In 1834 John sold his land inheritance in Davidson Co. TN to William Gambill.[3]

Cases Prosecuted - May Term 1830
Postmaster General vs John McClellan, [   ] Rogers & Edward Gwin[4]
Debt
Defendants pay debt, damages and costs.

Postmaster General vs Thomas Edmondson and Nicholas Perkins, executors of Peter Perkins[5]
Debt
Plaintiff recovers $658.35.

Cases Prosecuted - November Term 1830
The United States vs William Estis[6]
Trespass $10,000
Defendant came not, jury awards plaintiff $8,225.40 plus costs.

On June 18, 1831 G. W. Collinsworth arrived in New Orleans from Brazoria on the Irish schooner *Nelson*. He was listed as a merchant, age 21.[7] George was likely on his way back to Nashville with news and dreams from Texas.

---

[1]. Register of the Officers and Cadets of the U.S. Military Academy, June 1830.
[2]. George W. Cullum, Biographical Register of the Officers and Graduates of the U.S. Military Academy, Vol. I, 1802-1840, (New York: D. Van Nostrand, 1868), pp 370-371.
[3]. Davidson Co. TN Deed Book X, p 400.
[4]. Final Record Books of the U.S. District Court in Nashville 1806-1850, pp 327-328.
[5]. Final Record Books of the U.S. District Court in Nashville 1806-1850, pp 328-329.
[6]. Final Record Books of the U.S. District Court in Nashville 1806-1850, p 334.
[7]. Quarterly Abstracts of Passenger Lists of Vessels Arriving at New Orleans, Louisiana, 1820–1875. M272, 17 rolls. Records of the U.S. Customs Service, Record Group 36. National Archives and Records Administration, Washington, D.C.

In 1831 James' attorney friend, James I. Dozier, became mired in debt to several individuals and companies. Dozier constructed a deed of trust to secure his debts, conveying to James what may have been all his personal possessions, including his law library. Evidently, Dozier did not pay the installments called for in the deed of trust and Dozier's library became the basis for James' highly regarded law library.

James Collinsworth of James I. Dozier
Deed of Trust – signed September 19, 1831 Registered May 16, 1832

James I. Dozier is indebted to John R. Burke, Timothy W. Gilman, Samuel Tilford, Gowdy & Brenan, James Bell, John D. Goss, Charles Pugsley, Jno. M. Hill, Doyle & Eastland, David Thompson, Boyd McNairy, Austin Gresham and to secure the above debts does convey the following property:
Bacon's *Abridgment*, 7 volumes, Coke's *Commentaries*, 3 Vols., Comyn's *Digest*, 8 V., Kent's *Commentaries*, 3 V, Chitty's *Pleadings*, 3 V, Shepard's *Touchstone*, 2 V, *Revised Code Criminal Review*, Criminal Digest, Blackstone's *Commentaries*, 4V, Bingham on *Infancy*, Land Laws, Powell on *Contracts*, Chitty on *Bills*, Harrison's *Chancery*, 2 V, Cruise's *Digest* 7 V, Haywood & Cobbs *Digest* 2 V, Hawkins *Pleas of the Crown*, Maddox *Chancery* 2 V, Comyn on *Contracts*, 2 V, Boscawen on *The Statutes*, Noy's *Maxims*, Barton's *Equity*, Jones on *Bailment*, Roberts on *Frauds*, Kyd on *Awards*, Mitford's *Pleadings*, Espinass's, 2 V, Sullivan's Lectures, 2 V, Montesquire's *Spirit of Laws*, 2 V, Herring's *Justices*, Montague on *Set Off*, Reeve's *Domestic Relations*, Selwyn's *Nisi pries*, 2 V, Philip's *Evidence*, Starkie's *Evidence*, 3 V, Archbold's *Criminal Law*, Toller's *Law of Executors*, *Laws of Kentucky*, 2 V, *Laws of United States*, 2 V, *Condensed Reports* 3V, Cooke's *Reports*, 8V, Cromyn's Report, 2 V, Saunders Reports, 3 V, Atkyn's Reports, 3 V, Haardin's *Reports*, Bibbs' *Reports*, 4 V, Marshall's *Reports, 3 V,* Herring & Munford's *Reports*, 4 V, Littell's *Reports*, 6 V, Durnford & East, 8 V, Salkeld's *Reports*, 3 V, Washington's *Reports*, 2V, Douglass *Reports*, 2 V, Vesey Jr. *Reports*, 24 V, *English Common Law Reports*, 18 V, Large Family Bible, Scott's Family Bible, Blair's Sermons, Buck's Theological Dictionary, Webster's Dictionary, Johnson's Dictionary, Bailey's Dictionary, Hume's *History of England*, 12V, Anacharsis' *History of Greece*, 4 V, Gillie's *History of Greece*, 5 V, Rollings *Ancient History*, 8 V, *Casket*, 3 V, *Encyclopedia*, 12 V, *Shakespeare's Plays*, 12 V, Ewell's *Medical Companion* & Pike's *Expedition*.

One negro woman, named Aggy, two cows, three beds, bedsteads & furniture, one small trundle bed, one fine gold patent leather watch chain & seal, one silver watch, one sideboard and the following articles of cut glass, two large pitchers, two small pitchers, 2 large

Chapter 4: The President Appoints an Attorney

decanters, 2 small decanters, two dozen tumblers, two dozen wine glasses, two large bowls, one cordial stand, one dozen large silver spoons, half dozen teaspoons, one set of dining tables, one bureau, one breakfast table, three small tables, one dozen chairs, Windsor, half dozen office chairs, one office table, one office bookcase, water cart and gear, yankee clock, two large looking glasses, two small looking glasses, three pair brass andirons, two pair iron andirons, two pair tongs & 2 shovels, one fire fender, one set of china, 80 pieces, four large waiters, 4 small waiters, four large Liverpool dishes, one dozen plates, one castor, candlestand, wash stand, three pots, 3 ovens, two skillets, & griddle & grid iron, two fire grates, four trunks, 1 axe, 2 hoes, rifle gun, two five gallon demijons, one large stone, one small secretary & two carpets, one of thirty six and one of 24 yards. In Trust - if paid off in installments this deed to be void, Dozier reserves right to retain & use the possession.

19 Sept. 1831 James I. Dozier
Test: J. B. Mullen, James W. Bacon

On November 28, 1831 James was witness to a deed of trust for five slaves, Robert B. Turner to James B. Williams, two of his clients.[1]

Cases Prosecuted - May Term 1831
The Post Master General vs James A Henderson[2]
Debt
Defendants pay debt, damages and costs.

Recording of a letter affirming a patent[3] for an improved plow and granting a fourteen year term beginning April 12, 1831, signed by Andrew Jackson, Martin Van Buren, Secretary of State, and _____ _____ Secretary of State.

The Postmaster General of the United States vs Levi Holland, appearance bond of William Bloodworth [4]
Continuation of a case from May 1828. $700.00
Letter from President of the United States to the Marshall of West Tennessee District.

---

[1]. Davidson Co. TN Deed Book T, p 450.
[2]. Final Record Books of the U.S. District Court in Nashville 1806-1850, p 330.
[3]. Final Record Books of the U.S. District Court in Nashville 1806-1850, pp 332-333.
[4]. Final Record Books of the U.S. District Court in Nashville 1806-1850, p 338.

Postmaster General of the United States vs James W Combs, Aaron V Brown and Levi H Brown[1]
Debt $500 Continuation of a case from November term 1830.
Jury awarded plaintiff the sum of $357.33 plus costs.

The United States of America vs Hugh Moore[2]
Debt /Trespass $3,000.00 continuation of a case from November term 1830.
Jury awards plaintiff $2,047.50 plus costs.

Cases Prosecuted - November Term 1831
The United States of America vs The Nashville Bank[3]
Trespass $10,000, continuation of case from November 1830

Postmaster General of the United States vs Joseph Simmons and Isaac Sampson[4]
Debt $100.00
Plaintiff to recover $135.87 plus $15.75 damages

Postmaster General of the United States vs Hezekiah Bradbury and John Pool[5]
Debt $500.00 continuation of a case of 1828
Plaintiff to recover the debt plus $195.74 damages plus costs.

Postmaster General vs John Stul, Alexander Rogers and Solomon Hunt[6]
Debt $800.00 plus damages $100.00, continued from 1828.
Plaintiff to recover the debt plus $241.17 in damages.

Postmaster General vs Jesse Simpson[7]
Debt $300.00 plus $100.00 damages from a debt in 1825
[Resolution unreadable]

---

[1]. Final Record Books of the U.S. District Court in Nashville 1806-1850, pp 339-341.
[2]. Final Record Books of the U.S. District Court in Nashville 1806-1850, pp 342-343.
[3]. Final Record Books of the U.S. District Court in Nashville 1806-1850, pp 335-337.
[4]. Final Record Books of the U.S. District Court in Nashville 1806-1850, pp 343-344.
[5]. Final Record Books of the U.S. District Court in Nashville 1806-1850, p 345.
[6]. Final Record Books of the U.S. District Court in Nashville 1806-1850, pp 346-347.
[7]. Final Record Books of the U.S. District Court in Nashville 1806-1850, pp 347-348.

Chapter 4: The President Appoints an Attorney

Postmaster General vs John Parker and Felix Parker[1]
Debt $500.00 note date 1826
Jury determines plaintiff to recover debt plus $298.77 damages.

Postmaster General vs John Parker and John Wilson[2]
Debt $500.00 note dated 1825
Jury determines plaintiff to recover debt plus $316.00 damages plus costs.

Chickasaw Treaty of 1818 revisited in 1832 as an attempted scandal[3]

This treaty, by the terms of which the Chickasaw Indians ceded that part of the States of Tennessee and Kentucky lying-west of the Tennessee River to the United States, was negotiated in the year 1818 by Gen. Andrew Jackson, of Tennessee, and Gov. Isaac Shelby, of Kentucky, commissioners on the part of the United States. It was ratified by the United States Senate in January, 1819.

Years before this date, citizens of the State heard from hunters and trappers that there was a great salt mine on one of the tributaries of the Tennessee River, and efforts had been made to acquire the privilege from the Indian owners of working it. They had been led to believe that a salt mine was located on the territory of which they were proprietors; and when negotiations were inaugurated for its cession, the Indians demanded a reservation that should embrace it. Their wishes were met by the fourth article of the treaty by setting aside an area 4 miles square, approximately 10,000 acres, to be leased to a citizen of the United States who would pay the Indian Nation annually in bushels of salt. If sufficient salt was not present the lease shall be forfeited and the reservation revert to the United States.

The day following its ratification, and months before its ratification by the Senate, the two chiefs, Colbert and Brown, leased the reservation to Maj. William B. Lewis, of Nashville, for the benefit of himself and R. P. Currin, of Franklin, Tenn., for the term of 199 years for the consideration of 750 bushels of salt per annum. The contract provided that in case the salt water on this reservation and above-recited premises, upon a fair experiment being made, shall be found not to be of quality and quantity sufficient to justify the working thereof, then and in that case the aforesaid agreement to be void and of no effect.

This lease gave rise to an unfounded scandal involving the honor of General Jackson; it was the fact that Major Lewis was conveniently present

---

[1]. Final Record Books of the U.S. District Court in Nashville 1806-1850, pp 343-349.
[2]. Final Record Books of the U.S. District Court in Nashville 1806-1850, pp 349-350.
[3]. James D. Porter: The Chickasaw Treaty of 1818, A V Goodpasture, Editor, *American Historical Magazine and Tennessee Historical Society Quarterly, Vol. IX,* (Nashville: Goodpasture Book Co., 1904), pp 252-256.

and was a witness to the treaty. He had been Jackson's aid-de-camp at New Orleans, and was his closest friend. He secured the lease the day following its execution; and his associate, Mr. Currin, at once entered upon the work of developing the salt mine. General Jackson never suspected wrong from any of his friends; it was next to impossible to shake his confidence in them. He would rather have suffered injustice than to believe that in a pecuniary transaction they would connive at his injury.

Mr. Currin, at an expense of $3,000, bored the great artesian well of Henry County, the first of its kind known to the writer. He introduced salt workers from the Kanawha District and fixtures for the conversion of salt. The salt mine did not exist, and his efforts and expenditures resulted in failure.

This reservation was situated in what is now Henry County and, upon the settlement of the county, was entered and granted and occupied according to the laws of the State. No cognizance was taken of any right acquired under the lease from the Chickasaws to Major Lewis; but in the year 1830 interest in the reservation was renewed, and the scandal of 1818 was revived, to the injury of General Jackson, now President of the United States. It was now that Gen. John Coffee, of Alabama, and Maj. John H. Eaton, of Tennessee, Secretary of War in the Cabinet of President Jackson, were appointed commissioners on the part of the United States to negotiate treaties with the Choctaw and Chickasaw Indians for the purpose of extinguishing their title to the territory occupied by them in Alabama and Mississippi and to prepare for their removal to the territory provided for them west of the Territory of Arkansas.

The commissioners met a delegation of chiefs and head men at Franklin, Tenn., at which General Jackson was present, and agreed upon a treaty. It was agreed that Lewis and Currin should have an estate in the reservation for the period of 199 years, which was equivalent to a title in fee simple. The lease would run to the year 2029. The lessees were to pay the Indians $2,500 in cash and four bushels of salt per annum. Without waiting for the ratification of the treaty, Lewis and Currin had it recorded as an ordinary title paper.

The scandal continued; Major Eaton was a Cabinet officer; Major Lewis was his brother-in-law, and was second auditor of the United States Treasury; and Mr. Currin was the business partner of another brother-in-law. The reservation was productive and very valuable for farming purposes. Discussion of the sale was transferred from the people and press to Washington. Mr. Ellsworth, a distinguished Representative in Congress from Connecticut, attacked it in a speech: "The transaction was suspicious, and needs explanation. What had the commissioners to do with the matter of Mr. Lewis? They were sent to buy land from the Indians, not to sell land to white men. They must have known that Mr. Lewis had no title before, and here for $2,000 at a blow he acquired 10,000 acres of valuable land."

This is a forgotten incident; but at the time interest in it was so widespread that Hon. Edward Everett, of Massachusetts, then a

Chapter 4: The President Appoints an Attorney

Representative in Congress, offered this resolution: "*Resolved*, That the President of the United States be requested to communicate to this House a copy of the treaty negotiated with the Chickasaw tribe of Indians in the year 1830."

By January 1832 the treaty was in the hands of President Jackson. Representative Isaacks, of Tennessee, opposed the adoption of the resolution, "because, it was an invasion of the constitutional prerogatives of the Executive and his advisers." Mr. Everett consented to the postponement of the resolution for a day. On resuming its consideration, he delivered himself with force and power, and, referring to the commissioners and their action, said: "It is essentially corrupt, and the parties concerned in it have laid themselves under a responsibility which no Act of the Senate can remove."

The subject was finally referred to the House Committee on Public Lands to determine the facts. Because Mr. Charles Wycliffe, an enemy of the Jackson Administration, was named chair of the Committee and further had employed a relative of his, Mr. Tobin, to take depositions of people who lived in the area of the reservation, Jackson became very worried about this sequence of events. Some of Jackson's allies on the Committee succeeded in including James Collinsworth into the fray by appointing him to join Mr. Tobin in taking the depositions to avoid a one-sided investigation. Jackson expresses his anger and his fears in a letter[1] to his friend, General Coffee:

Washington, March 13, 1832

(Private)
My D'r Genl,

I am just informed this evening that the committee on public lands, at whose head is Mr. Charles Wyckliffe, has directed a messenger to go on to Tennessee to take depositions as to the value of the reserve including the salt spring, and to bring on copies of the lease etc, etc., and that a cousin of Mr. Wyckliffe is selected, a violent opposer [sic] of the administration, to perform this service. Mr. Clay of Alabama, one of the committee, has had Mr. Colinsworth [sic] added to this commission, beginning to think, that there is more under the rose than is seen—Wycklift [sic]it is well understood here has gone over to the enemy.

It may be that it is intended to implicate you and Major Eaton, and perhaps reach others. It may be that as Doctor McNairy has been here, James Jackson is to be interrogated. If that is the case, have Col. McKinley sworn as to the conversation he had with James Jackson on this subject, on the receipt of this see and converse with Col McKinley on this subject. Col. McKinley well remembers that

---

[1]. John Spencer Bassett Ed., *Correspondence of Andrew Jackson, Vol. IV*, (Washington DC, The Carnegie Institution of Washington, 1929), pp 417-418.

James told him that I had no knowledge of the lease being obtained by Major Lewis until I reached Nashville.

It cannot be possible, that if there were nothing in this but to obtain information of the value of the land that a special messenger would be sent at the expence [sic] of four dollars a day and his expences [sic], a violent enemy and cousin of Wyckliffs. The instructions to Colinsworth [sic] is to notify Mr. Currin, but who knows what may be the private instructions of Wyckliff (who has turned traitor) to this agent of Chiltons, and violent enemy of this administration. I write this to put you on your guard, the stroke is intended at you and Eaton, and thereby if possible to effect [sic] me, therefore it will be proper if James Jackson is called upon, to be present yourself, and have Col McKinley present to interrogate [sic] him.

Hutchings is now with me, he came today. I will send him home. I am surrounded with traitors, but I fear not, I will with the aid of providence, put all down. In haste, with my love to Polly and the family.

       I am yr friend
       Andrew Jackson
P. S. let me know if this reaches you.

The Committee, through its chairman Mr. Wickliffe of Kentucky, made its report reciting its findings. The substantial one was that Messrs. Lewis and Currin had acquired no title to the reservation and that it was subject to entry and grant upon the same terms and conditions as other territory acquired under the treaty of 1818. Mr. Wickliffe moved to communicate the report and accompanying documents to the Senate. Under the leadership of John Bell, the motion was denied. Mr. Wickliffe's purpose was to defeat the ratification of the treaty by furnishing Senators with the facts; but it died in the President's office, and that was the extinguishment of the title of Messrs. Lewis and Currin.

Cases Prosecuted - May Term 1832

Postmaster General vs Benj. Wright, Thomas Lane and William Beaty[1]
Debt $500.00 note dated 1825
Jury determines plaintiff to recover debt plus $316.00 damages plus costs.
 On November 1, 1832 George W. Collinsworth granted to James his power of attorney to sell his Lot 1 of their father's estate.[2]

---

[1]. Final Record Books of the U.S. District Court in Nashville 1806-1850, pp 351-352.
[2]. Davidson Co. TN Deed Book V, pp 20-21.

The Ross Concession: Unbelievable Opportunity or Colossal Hoax? [1]

Just a month later James became aware of a "business opportunity" that surely opened his eyes to potential wealth and fame in Texas:

"Beginning at the point West at which terminates the Colony of Gen. Arthur A Wevell, upon the Red River of Nachitoches; from thence running up the said River, the South side thereof, with its meanders, passing the South-west corner of Arkansas Territory, to a point on said River, where the one hundred and second degree of west Longitude from London crosses it; from thence South, with said degree, twenty leagues; from thence East, parallel with the said Red River, two hundred and twenty miles, to the west boundary of said Wevell's grant, thence North with said boundary to the beginning; including *eighteen millions four hundred thousand acres*, (18,400,000)."

Thus read the May 1,1828 description of a "supposed" Mexican government land grant to General Reuben Ross[2] of Tennessee, on which he in return was obligated to settle 200 families, one-third of them Mexican, by May 1, 1834. Anxious either to meet his settlers' obligation or to sell his grant we are not told which, Ross set out for the United States. En route, in July 1828, he was murdered, having had no chance to either register his grant in Tennessee or to transfer it to other parties, thus title remained in the Mexican government.

In 1832 a group of entrepreneurs in Nashville emerged under the title of the "Ross Company" for the purpose of securing financial gain from the Ross Concession. The President and Members were: John Shelby, president, W[ashington] Barrow, Jno. C. McLemore, Andrew Hynes, Robert H. McEwen, Matthew Waston, Joseph Vaulx, and S. B. Marshall & Co. Neither their relationship to Reuben Ross nor the nature of their claim to the Ross Concession is established by the record.

The strategy of the Ross Company, just in case there was any credibility to the supposed grant, was to contract, without substantial investment, with a man "in whose capacity and integrity" they "have full faith and credit, to proceed forthwith to any part of the Mexican republic he may please for the purpose of obtaining confirmation of the grant issued to the said Reuben Ross...."

---

[1]. *Historic Maury Co. TN Quarterly Journal Vol. XXXI*, No 2, pp 122-124.

[2]. Reuben Ross, a native of Virginia, was a member of the Gutiérrez-Magee expedition from May 1812 to June 16, 1813. At the battle of Rosillo on March 29, 1813, Ross and Samuel Kemper routed the Spanish forces by leading a furious charge. Ross became the senior Anglo-American officer with the expedition after Kemper's departure, but Ross himself left the army in June 1813.

On September 22, 1832, the Ross Company entered into a contract with General William Arnold.[1] He had broad powers: 1) accept modification or extension of time; 2) exchange it for another of equal value; 3) or change and remodel the grant. In consideration of his services, Arnold was to receive one half of the grant, if confirmed, or "one half of whatever" he obtained.

Arnold, either feeling confident that he would secure some land, or entering into the spirit of an alleged fraud, immediately proceeded to offer one million acres (1,000,000) for sale in 400 shares of 2,500 acres each, the selling price $250 per share, or 10 cents per acre. Arnold prepared and numbered scrip which were distributed widely to his agents. One such scrip, No. 196, was issued on 13 October 1832, several months before Arnold began his fateful trip to Mexico, to one Parry Washington Porter of Maury County, Tennessee, Porter paying by giving his "restricted" note on Arnold's agreement to place the note with Porter's brother, Thomas Jefferson Porter, as holding agent until the grant was secured, and if not secured, same to be given up to its maker.

Arnold's purpose was getting money "in hand." Barely two months after receiving Porter's note, it was transferred on December 10, 1832 to James Collinsworth, though it is alleged that the endorsement is not in the handwriting of either Arnold or Collinsworth. Then, a week later on December 17, 1832, the note is again transferred, this time by Collinsworth, in payment for merchandise purchases, to the Benson Hunt & Company. Again it is alleged that the endorsement is not in Collinsworth's handwriting. It is shown that Benson Hunt & Company is a wholesale/retail mercantile company of Nashville doing business with Hunt and Patterson, a wholesale mercantile company of Baltimore, Maryland.

To complete his part of the deal, in 1833 Arnold resigned his commission as Major-General of the Tennessee militia, and relocated his family to Texas, where he received a land grant of 4428 acres (not related to the Ross Concession) in Austin's Colony in Brazoria County, recorded on April 15,

---

[1]. In 1813 Lieut. William Arnold, of the 39th Regiment of Regulars, was sent to Kingston, TN, to recruit for the war; one of his recruits was Pvt. Sam Houston, future Governor of Tennessee and of Texas. William was admitted in 1820 to practice law at Kingston, Roane County, Tennessee. In 1821 he was appointed Commissioner for laying out the city of Jackson in Madison County, TN. In 1825, Col. William Arnold was elected Major-General of the Old Third Division, Tennessee Militia, by a vote of 25 to 16 over Col. Robert Dyer. In 1826 he ran for public office and was defeated by Davy Crockett. In the years 1827-1831 he accumulated numerous debts, prompting his interest in profitable business deals. On September 22, 1832 Gen. Arnold signed contract with the Ross Company to go to TX to investigate claims of land ceded to Ruben Ross by the Mexican Government. [Williams, *Historic Madison: Militia and the Seminole War*, p. 100.]

Chapter 4: The President Appoints an Attorney

1833. He died unexpectedly on June 9, 1833, Velasco, Brazoria County, Texas.

Soon after Arnold's death, and still laboring under the 6-year termination clause in the Ross Grant, the Ross Company claimed that Arnold's interest in the Concession, and thus his scrip, was null and void because he had not performed his part of the contract. The Company then advertised, calling for all scrip holders to render payment of $20 per scrip "or they would not be recognized as claimants." This action launched a lawsuit in the Maury County Chancery Court that would not be resolved until April 7, 1837.

There is no evidence that the Ross Concession was ever consummated. Later, James would be the administrator of Arnold Ross' estate in Brazoria County, Texas.

Cases Prosecuted - November Term 1832
The Postmaster General of the United States vs Richard W. Morris, Beverly Guthrie and George Smith[1]
Debt $800 Continuation of a case from December 1826.
Defendant came not, plaintiff to recover debt plus $101.47 damages.

The Postmaster General of The United States vs Jacob Tipton and Michael H [unreadable][2]
Debt $500 Continuation of a case from October 1832
Defendant came not, plaintiff to recover debt of $500.00.

The Postmaster General of the United States vs Jacob Tipton and John L. Brown[3]
Debt $700 Continuation of a case from February 1824.
Defendant came not, Plaintiff to recover debt plus $352.89 damages.

On Friday February 22, 1833 James' brother, George W. Collinsworth Esq., counselor and attorney at law, came into Court, took the oaths required by law and was admitted to practice in this Court [Franklin, Williamson Co. TN].[4]

---

[1]. Final Record Books of the U.S. District Court in Nashville 1806-0850, p 361.
[2]. Final Record Books of the U.S. District Court in Nashville 1806-1850, p 362.
[3]. Final Record Books of the U.S. District Court in Nashville 1806-1850, p 362.
[4]. Williamson Co TN Circuit Court Minutes Vol. 7, p 364.

Cases Prosecuted - May Term 1833
Postmaster General vs Benj. Wright, Thomas Lane and William Beaty[1]
Debt $500.00 note dated 1825
Jury determines plaintiff to recover debt plus $316.00 damages plus costs.

Postmaster General vs James Bradley, executor of Thomas Roberts, James McManey, and Charles Grady.[2]
Debt $500.00 continuation of case from January term 1829.
Defendants came not, plaintiff to recover debt plus $201.66 damages.

Postmaster General vs Henry Crabb, Executor, Harry L. Douglas and Jane, his wife and John Bell Executor of Henry Crabb, dec'd[3]
Debt $2000 continuation of case from November 1832
Case transferred to Circuit court of the United States for the District of West Tennessee.

The Post Master General of the United States vs Charles Finkles[4]
Debt $700 Continuation from January 1826
The matters and things being seen and understood; it is adjudged that said demurer be overruled, and said plaintiff not further prosecuting his said suit; It is considered by the court that the defendant go hence without delay.

After James' sister Parmelia and Lloyd Davis had been married about 10 years and were raising three small children, their indebtedness became too much to handle. Her brothers, George and James, as partners formed a deed of trust on October 15, 1833 securing Lloyd and Parmelia's belongings, removing the property to George's land:

George Collinsworth of Loyd Davis

Deed of Trust -   Registered Oct 15, 1833

Loyd Davis sells to George Collinsworth the following parcels of property: 1 chesnut [sic]sorrel horse,1 bright sorrel horse, 1 dun mare & colt, 1 sorrel mare, 1 dun colt, 1 sorrel colt, 2 yoke steers & oxcart, 3 cows & yearlings, 35 head of sheep, 80 barrels of corn, 2000 bundles of fodder, 460 dozen of oats, 1 bureau & Jackson press,

---

[1]. Final Record Books of the U.S. District Court in Nashville 1806-1850, pp 351-352.
[2]. Final Record Books of the U.S. District Court in Nashville 1806-1850. p372.
[3]. Final Record Books of the U.S. District Court in Nashville 1806-1850 p373.
[4]. Final Record Books of the U.S. District Court in Nashville 1806-1850, p366.

> *3 beds & bedsteads & furniture, 45 head of hogs, cooking utensils & castings, 1 clock, 1 small bureau & table, ploughs, hoes & other farming utensils and 1000 pounds of bacon. Subject to trusts and conditions: said Loyd Davis owes Wm. Black, Shall & Cantrell, J. Maxwell, John Dabbs, Adm. of --- Hoover, B. Spence, tanner, H. Hagans, Alfred Balch, for professional services. All the foregoing property being now on the land of said George Collinsworth, held by him in partnership with his brother.*
> *L. Davis*
> *Test: Bethel Norman[1]*

Only four days later at a public sale conducted by the sheriff[2], James purchased the stock, household goods and a slave girl that had been put in trust:

> *James Collinsworth of Willoughby Williams Sheriff*
> *Bill of Sale - Registered 21 July 1835*
>
> *I, Willoughby Williams, Sheriff of Davidson Co., by virtue of said office, did expose to public sale, on the 19th of October 1833, the following property, levied on by virtue of an execution in favour [sic]of James Collinsworth, as the property of Loyd Davis: Three head of horses, two yoke of steers, fourteen head of cattle, thirty eight head of hogs, thirty five head of sheep, five beds and other household furniture, and one negro girl, named Martha, about twelve or thirteen years of age. James Collinsworth became the purchaser of all of said property.*
>
> *I, Willoughby Williams, Sheriff, do hereby sell & deliver to James Collinsworth, all the right, title & interest of the said Loyd Davis.*
>
> *20 Feb 1835 Willo. Williams, Shff.*

James held this property for about two years. According to family legend, Lloyd and Parmelia spent this period in Alabama because of her health, the cost of which could have contributed to their indebtedness.

Cases Prosecuted - November Term 1833
Postmaster General vs Benj. Wright, Thomas Lane and William Beaty[3]
Debt $500.00 note dated 1825
Jury determines plaintiff to recover debt plus $316.00 damages plus costs.

---

[1]. Davidson Co. TN Deed Book W, p 67.
[2]. Davidson Co. TN Deed Book W, p 643.
[3]. Final Record Books of the U.S. District Court in Nashville 1806-1850, pp 351-352.

James' appointment to be United States Attorney for the District of West Tennessee apparently was a five year term. When that time passed, he was reappointed by Andrew Jackson:

Washington, February 14, 1834.
To the Senate of the United States:

I nominate James Collinsworth to be attorney of the United States for the western district of Tennessee, from the 16th instant, when his present commission expired.

Andrew Jackson[1]

Cases Prosecuted - May Term 1834

<u>Postmaster General vs Benj. Wright, Thomas Lane and William Beaty</u>[2]
Debt $500.00 note dated 1825
Jury determines plaintiff to recover debt plus $316.00 damages plus costs.

<u>The Post Master General of the</u> United States vs Felix McConnell, William Edmiston and Elliott H. Fletcher[3]
Debt $1500 Continuation of a case from August 1830
Defendants came not, plaintiff to recover debt plus $713.75 damages.

<u>The United States of America vs John L. Campbell</u>[4]
Debt $425 and damages of $100
Plaintiff will no further prosecute. Plaintiff to recover of the defendant the costs by him assumed.

<u>The Post Master General vs E. A. Tanant, John A. Wilson & Jno T. Harman</u>[5]
Debt $500 and damages of $100.00 Continuation of a case from March 1830
And the said defendants by their attorney on the 28 May 1834 filed the following plea vs The Post Master General: E. A. Tanant, John A. Wilson and John T. Harmon by attorney come and defend the ... pleas say that the said post master General of the United States ought not to have and maintain his said action against them because they say that they have well and truly

---

[1]. Journal of the Executive Proceedings of the Senate of the United States of America, 1829-1837, Wednesday, February 14, 1834, p 357.
[2]. Final Record Books of the U.S. District Court in Nashville 1806-1850, pp 351-352.
[3]. Final Record Books of the U.S. District Court in Nashville 1806-1850, p 367.
[4]. Final Record Books of the U. S. District Court in Nashville 1806-1850, pp 367-368.
[5]. Final Record Books of the U.S. District Court in Nashville 1806-1850, p368.

Chapter 4: The President Appoints an Attorney

kept and performed the said condition in the writing obligation in all things by them to be kept.

On July 19, 1834 James is listed among notes due by Edwin H. Ewing, trustee in bankruptcy of the firm of Cantrell and Allen.[1]

Case Prosecuted - November Term 1834
The Post Master General vs Samuel Morgan, James D. Thomas and Abraham Hall[2]
Debt $300 Continuation of a case from Sept. 1829
Defendants came not, plaintiffs to recover debt plus $73.25 damages.

Preparing to Relocate to Texas
On January 25, 1835 James resigned as United States Attorney for the District of West Tennessee in a simple letter to President Jackson:

Nashville
25th Jan 1835

To the The President of the U. States

Sir
After returning my grateful acknowledgement for the partiality manifested in having appointed me to fill the office of attorney of the U. States for the District of West Tennessee you will be pleased to consider this as my resignation of the same.

Very Respectfully Your
Obedient Servant
James Collinsworth

---

[1]. Davidson Co. TN Deed Book W, p 453.
[2]. Final Record Books of the U.S. District Court in Nashville 1806-1850, p 371.

> at Dept. of State
> Feb. 2. 1835
>
> Nashville
> 28th Jan. 1835
>
> Sir,
>
> The President of the U. States
>
> Sir, After returning my grateful acknowledgements for the partiality manifested, in having heretofore appointed me to fill the office of attorney of the U. States for the district of West Tennessee. You will be pleased to consider this as my resignation of the same.
>
> Very Respectfully your
> Obedient Servant
> Ja^s Collinsworth

Chapter 4: The President Appoints an Attorney

In February 1835 James acted as attorney in fact for brother George in sale of 28 acres for $300 to William Gambill[1] as brother John had done a year earlier. This land was George's inheritance from his father. It is quite likely that George had already removed to Texas.

In a final gesture toward securing the financial future of Lloyd and Parmelia Davis before he left for Texas, James created a trust that contained his share of his mother's estate plus their property he had bought at public sale. He named James P. H. Grundy, his good friend and son of Felix Grundy, then U.S. Senator, as trustee to administer the trust to their benefit:

Deed of Trust - James Collinsworth, James P H Grundy and Parmelia A Davis[2]

Registered February 21, 1835

This indenture this day made and entered into between James Collinsworth of the first part and James P H Grundy of the second part and Parmelia A Davis of the third part witnesseth; that the said James Collinsworth for and in consideration of the sum of five dollars to him in hand paid, the receipt of which is hereby acknowledged, as well as the consideration hereinafter mentioned, has this day bargained and sold,_____, _____ and conveyed to the said James P H Grundy the following property, viz, all his right, title and interest to his undivided part of a tract of land in Davidson County on the waters of Mill Creek, being the property of Alice Collinsworth at the time of her death, also one negro girl named Martha about thirteen years of age. Also all the property, stock and household furniture purchased by me at a sale where I was plaintiff and Loyd Davis defendant, which property will more fully appear by reference to the Sheriff's return and bill of sale to me. To have and to hold to the said James P H Grundy for the following purposes and trusts, that is to say, the aforesaid property is conveyed expressly for the purpose of affording support and sustinance to the said Parmeila A Davis wife of Loyd Davis and the children she now has or may hereafter have; and it is the understanding & object of this trust that the said James P H Grundy is to allow the said Loyd Davis and his wife and children to use said property for the support of himself his wife and the children of his wife so long as they live together as husband and wife in such manner as said trustee may deem most advisable. Any remainder in said property to belong to said Parmelia A Davis and her heirs and distributees forever. And it is expressly understood and agreed ___ that said James P H Grundy is not to be rendered personally liable for any waste, mismanagement or other injury done to said property by the use

---

[1]. Davidson Co. TN Deed Book X, pp 480-481.
[2]. Davidson Co. TN Deed Book X, p 495.

occupation or other acts done by the said Loyd Davis or his wife in regard to said property. Witness my hand this _____ day of February 1835.

Jas. Collinsworth {seal}

State of Tennessee Davidson County __ Personally appeared before me Jacob McGavock clerk of the circuit court for Davidson County the within named James Collinsworth the bargainer with whom I am personally acquainted, and who acknowledged that he executed the within deed of trust for the purposed therein contained. Witness my hand at office this 21st February 1835.

Near the end of February 1835, James removed to Brazoria, Texas to set up his law practice and seek his fortune there.

Chapter 5 - Stirring Up Flames of Revolution

Before James Collinsworth resigned his Nashville appointment as United States Attorney for the District of West Tennessee, others of his family had preceded him to Texas. His first cousins, brothers George Morse Collinsworth[1] and David Cook Collinsworth, and his younger brother, George Washington Collinsworth, also an attorney, already were there. James left his home in Nashville for Brazoria where he planned to use his experience as United States Attorney for the District of West Tennessee in the Texian struggle for independence. Headright Certificate No. 83 issued to him January 25, 1838 for one-third of a league of land by the Board of Land Commissioners for Brazoria County simply states that he came to Texas previous to May 2, 1835.[2]

The route most likely taken by James was by boat from Nashville down the Cumberland River to the Ohio River, down the Ohio to the Mississippi River, then down the Mississippi to New Orleans. The last leg of his journey was from New Orleans by ship to the Port of Velasco at the mouth of the Brazos River, the gateway to the Anglo-American Settlements. At the municipality of Brazoria, some twenty miles upriver, James settled and established his law practice. A large part of his baggage on this circuitous journey was his treasured law library.

Brazoria County Texas in the early 1830s was sparsely populated. At the mouth of the Brazos River was the inn of Goodwin Brown Cotton, who had previously founded The Texas Gazette at San Felipe. Fifteen miles further up stream was the plantation of Greenville's McNeil and Thomas Westhall. At the town of Brazoria lots of 1/8 acre were selling for $20 to $120, depending on the location. The whole town hummed with activity. Board was obtained for $4.00 per week, the accommodations consisting of two

---

[1]. George Morse Collinsworth was a soldier, planter, and civil servant. Born in Mississippi in 1810, he was living in Brazoria, Texas, in 1832, when he participated in the battle of Velasco. In July of that year he was serving as secretary of the Brazoria Committee of Vigilance. On December 11, 1835, the General Council elected George M. Collinsworth collector of customs for the port of Matagorda. His resignation from the army was accepted on January 4, 1836. On January 12, 1838, he received a bounty warrant for 320 acres for his military service. He was nominated collector for the port of Matagorda on May 22, 1837 and subsequently several other civil service positions in Matagorda. Collinsworth married Susan R. Kendrick on June 5, 1837, in Matagorda County, where they lived until about 1854. In 1857 he was a surveyor in Karnes County. He died in Matagorda County on April 18, 1866. [http://www.tshaonline.org/handbook/online/articles/fco29 Accessed 3/4/2011]

[2]. Fannin County First Class Headright, File No. 909.

square log houses about fifteen feet apart with a covered passage way between where meals were served.[1]

By 1832 Brazoria was a town of some two or three hundred inhabitants situated on the right bank of the Brazos River. There were two streets that ran parallel with the river. Brick stores, frame buildings and a boarding house completed the picture.[2] In comparison, although still a frontier town, Nashville had a population well over 6,000 when James left.

By the end of 1834 General Antonio Lopez de Santa Anna had created a Mexican dictatorship and had repealed the 1824 Mexican Constitution. Tension was rising all across Texas due to the power Santa Anna had seized and the increasing number of Mexican soldiers in the area to quell any hint of rebellion.

James signed a petition drawn up at Brazoria on August 9, 1835, urging the call of a convention to declare the independence of Texas, thus beginning his journey of "stirring up the flames of revolution." In October of 1835 the simmering sentiments between Texans and Mexicans began to flare up in towns across the south of Texas, beginning about 70 miles east of San Antonio, in the town of Gonzales.

Gonzales: 10/2/1835[3]

Mexican troops under General Martin Perfecto Cos had originally landed at Copano Bay near Gonzales about September 20, 1835 and had marched into San Antonio. From there Lt. Castaneda and a force of about 100 troops were sent to recover a bronze cannon in Gonzales. When they arrived on September 29, they were surprised by eighteen local citizens who refused to let them cross the Guadalupe River. The Texians created a banner with a crude drawing of the disputed cannon and the words "Come and take it" written on it. Since they had no cannon balls, they filled it with scrap metal and fired it at the dragoons.

On the morning of October 2, 1835, the Texans, now comprising about 150 men, attacked the Mexican camp near the farm of Zeke Williams. Lt. Castaneda

---

[1]. Brazoria County Federation of Women's Clubs, *History of Brazoria County*, (Angleton TX: April, 1940) p 11.

[2]. Brazoria County Federation of Women's Clubs, *History of Brazoria County*, (Angleton TX: April, 1940) p 11.

[3]. Stephen L. Moore, *Savage Frontier; Rangers, Riflemen, and Indian Wars in Texas 1835-1837,* Vol. 1, University of North Texas Press, 2002, pp 31-32.

eventually removed his men back toward San Antonio de Bexar. The opening shots of the Texas Revolution had thus been fired in what became known as the Battle of Gonzales. The little town of Gonzales earned the sobriquet "Lexington of Texas."

Goliad: 10/9/1835[1]

Southeast of San Antonio toward the Gulf Coast, plenty was going on at Goliad, where the next round of the Texas Revolution occurred on October 9, 1835. Previously known as La Bahia, Goliad lay on the important route from the Gulf of Mexico to San Antonio de Bexar. La Bahia was crucial in that it guarded the principal supply line from the Port of Copano to San Antonio.

In early October 1835 Captain George Morse Collinsworth organized a company of men from the Matagorda area and marched to Victoria, picking up recruits along the way. General Cos had departed Goliad for San Antonio, leaving only a small garrison at the old Presidio La Bahia. Collinsworth eventually commanded about 120 men, including well-known former Mexican prisoner Benjamin Rush Milam. About 11 PM on October 9 the Texans captured the fortress at La Bahia in a half-hour assault while suffering only several wounded. The Mexicans lost three killed, seven wounded and twenty one made prisoners, including two senior officers.

On October 28 Capt. Fannin and his 90 man troop were victorious in a skirmish against a 275 man Mexican force near the Mission Conception. Early in the evening of October 29 a six-man Texas Army detachment was attacked by hostile Indians at a point about six miles from the Goliad fort. First Lt. David Collinsworth yelled out "Oh Lord" as he was hit and fell from his horse. Second Lt. Augustus H. Jones and the four other surviving company members rushed back to the fort. The following day they returned with eight others from their company and retrieved the body of Lt. Collinsworth. "He was shot in the neck and probably killed instantly," related Capt. Ingram. "The head and face bore several marks of savage violence." Lt. Collinsworth was buried "with the honors of war."

Days after the Gonzales and Goliad Battles, the provisional government of Texas assembled in San Felipe de Austin. Elections had been held on October 5 to elect fifty-five representatives from 13 jurisdictions or "municipalities" of Texas. These men began arriving in San Felipe for the opening session on October 15.

---

[1]. Stephen L. Moore, *Savage Frontier; Rangers, Riflemen, and Indian Wars in Texas 1835-1837,* Vol. 1, University of North Texas Press, 2002, pp 33, 48.

The Provisional Government at San Felipe[1] 11/1 - 11/14/1835

This convention was a meeting of Texas representatives to confer on the prerevolutionary quarrel with Mexico. There was not complete agreement on the power of this body. Some treated it as sovereign, but others insisted that the gathering was to investigate, counsel, and make recommendations to the people and denied that it could assume legislative or constitutional functions.

The provisional government set up by the Consultation was the only governing body in Texas from November 15, 1835, until March 1, 1836, and during much of the period it was inactive. Personalities entered into the dispute and after about a month the governor and the council quarreled bitterly. There was no agreement as to the powers of the governor. The council wished to cooperate with Mexican liberals; Gov. Smith wished to ignore the Declaration of November 7 and proceed as though Texas were an independent state.

As a result of the various controversies, the governor made an attempt to dissolve the council, which retaliated by impeaching Smith and recognizing Robinson as head of state. For all practical purposes the provisional government then ceased to exist, and Texas was without leadership during the critical month of February 1836. The government failed because the men responsible for it lost sight of the welfare of Texas in their personal quarrels.

There were many examples of the ineffectiveness of the provisional government: on the nomination of Mr. Wharton, the General Council of the Provisional Government on November 28, 1835, appointed James Collinsworth and George M. Collinsworth captains in the Texas Regiment of Infantry, a company that probably was never organized. And on December 13, 1835, Charles Wilson, judge at Matagorda, notified Governor Henry Smith that he had appointed James Collinsworth prosecuting attorney; but Wilson had no authority to make the appointment, and Collinsworth did not serve.

After James spoke at a meeting in Columbia on December 25, 1835, resolutions were presented recommending "to the people of the different Jurisdictions of Texas, the expediency of calling a new Convention of Texas with radical powers," and stating that "the time has now arrived when it is necessary to declare the total and absolute INDEPENDENCE OF TEXAS," and that "the Convention be instructed to form a Constitution for the Permanent Government of Texas, and submit the same to the people of the different Jurisdictions for their adoption- or rejection," and "that Edwin Waller, Esqr, be requested to present those resolutions to the Governor and Council and urge the adoption of the measures therein recommended."

---

[1]. Walter Prescott Webb, Editor-In-Chief, *Handbook of Texas, Vol 1*, (Austin: Texas State Historical Association, 1952), p 377.

Anson Jones and Election of Delegates to the Convention of 1836[1]

According to Anson Jones[2], "I took steps to aid in calling a public meeting of the citizens of the municipality or county of Brazoria, at Columbia. There was a large attendance. I drew up, offered, and advocated, as chairman of the committee, resolutions in favor of a 'Declaration of Independence from Mexico' and calling a Convention of the people of Texas on the first Monday in March, 1836, to make the Declaration, and to frame a Constitution."

"These recommendations were advocated by myself, J. Collinsworth, and B. C. Franklin, and opposed by W. J. Russell. Fearing to trust the vote, I proposed . . . the resolutions be signed by those who approved them, and go to the country as the expression of the individuals whose names should be appended. . . We succeeded in getting about twenty or thirty names from among those who were present; but . . . nearly everybody signed before they were published . . . The people of the country were at first startled by the boldness of the Columbia Resolutions, but . . . by the 2nd of March following, there were but few in the country who did not acquiesce in the propriety of the course proposed in those resolutions."

On February 1, 1836, Dr. Jones presided over Brazoria's polling place while his neighbors solemnly selected delegates "clothed with ample, unlimited, or plenary powers" to represent them in the Convention of the People of Texas at Washington-on-the-Brazos. The Governor and council had issued the election writs before their quarrels had paralyzed the provisional government.

---

[1]. Herbert Pickens Gambrell, *Anson Jones, The Last President of Texas, Second Edition*, (Austin: University of Texas Press, 1964), pp 54-59.

[2]. Anson Jones (1798–1858) wanted to be a printer but was persuaded to study medicine; 1820 he was licensed by the Oneida, New York, Medical Society. He met with meager success and soon moved to Norwich, where he opened a drugstore that failed. In 1824 he went to Venezuela for two years then returned to Philadelphia, opened a medical office, qualified for an M.D. degree at Jefferson Medical College in 1827. Again, his medical practice did not prosper. In October 1832 he renounced medicine and became a commission merchant in New Orleans, where he lived through cholera and yellow fever epidemics and a series of failures that left him despondent and broke. In October 1833, Jones drifted to Texas soon had a medical practice at Brazoria worth $5,000 a year. He joined in signing a petition for the calling of the Consultation but declined to be nominated as a delegate. When war came he enlisted and during the San Jacinto campaign was judge advocate and surgeon of the Second Regiment. Nevertheless, he insisted upon remaining a private in the infantry. [http://www.tshaonline.org/handbook/online/articles/fjo42 Accessed 3/15/2011]

Dr. Jones received five complimentary votes. He believed that he would have been one of the four Brazoria delegates, had he not "declined all requests to become a candidate," but he was then only "solicitous to give a right direction to affairs, and perfectly willing to let whoever wished have the carrying of them into execution."

Asa Brigham, James Collinsworth, Edwin Waller, and John S. D. Byrom were elected representatives of the Brazoria municipality. The votes of forty-seven recruits from New Orleans who had been in Texas less than five days helped to elect them.

During the month between the election and the opening of the convention, public sentiment everywhere veered unmistakably to independence, and there was no division of opinion on that question at Brazoria. Waller and Byrom, who had represented Brazoria in the Consultation that refused to decree separation from Mexico, received smaller votes than Brigham and Collinsworth who had never before participated in a public assembly in Texas.

James was named the first secretary of Holland Masonic Lodge at Brazoria in February, 1836. Two weeks after his election as representative, James was in court defending clients charged with murder:

Jurisdiction of Brazoria
Monday, February 15, 1836

Court in Session: }
L.C. Manson, P.J }
present:
the People of Texas
vs.
D. M'Lean }
J.T. Robinson. } Warrant for murder.

The said Dougald M'Lean and Jos. T. Robinson having been arrested under said charge therein set forth: after having the testimony in behalf of the people against the accused. On motion of Jas. Collinsworth Esq. they were discharged, not the slightest evidence before the Court calculated to produce the impression that they were any way concerned in or accessory to the murder of the individual for whose death they were arrested.

I certify the foregoing is a true extract from the record in my office.
L.C. Mason, Primary Judge[1]

---

[1] The Texas Republican. (Newspaper, Brazoria, TX), Vol. 2, No. 76, Ed. 1, Wednesday, March 2, 1836.

Chapter 5: Stirring Up Flames of Revolution

Beginning the Siege of the Alamo,[1] February 23, 1836

In December 1835, Ben Milam had led Texian and Tejano volunteers against Mexican troops quartered in the city. After five days of house-to-house fighting, they forced General Martín Perfecto de Cós and his soldiers to surrender. The victorious volunteers then occupied the Alamo — already fortified prior to the battle by Cós' men — and strengthened its defenses.

On February 23, 1836, the arrival of General Antonio López de Santa Anna's army outside San Antonio nearly caught them by surprise. Undaunted, the Texians and Tejanos prepared to defend the Alamo together. William B. Travis, the commander of the Alamo sent forth couriers carrying pleas for help to communities in Texas. On the eighth day of the siege, a band of 32 volunteers from Gonzales arrived, bringing the number of defenders to nearly two hundred. Legend holds that with the possibility of additional help fading, Colonel Travis drew a line on the ground and asked any man willing to stay and fight to step over — all except one did. As the defenders saw it, the Alamo was the key to the defense of Texas, and they were ready to give their lives rather than surrender their position to General Santa Anna. Among the Alamo's garrison were Jim Bowie, renowned knife fighter, and David Crockett, famed frontiersman and former congressman from Tennessee.

With the Alamo defenders under fierce siege, the scene quickly changes to Washington-on-the-Brazos where the representatives are in Convention to form a government for Texas.

---

[1]. http://www.thealamo.org/battle/battle.php Accessed 3/4/2011

Chapter 6 – Birth of the Republic of Texas

The Convention: March 1 – 17, 1836

The business of the Convention was conducted in an unfinished building, without doors or windows, which had been rented by a group of Washington [Texas], businessmen from gunsmith Noah Byars and real estate speculator Peter M. Mercer, for three months at $170. In place of glass, cotton cloth partly excluded the cold wind. On March 1, as the members convened, a norther came through, and by morning the temperature was 33 degrees.[1]

Replica of the building on the site where the Convention was held.

When the Convention began the Alamo already had been under siege for five days. The representatives hurriedly went about forming a government. <u>The proceedings in which James Collinsworth took an active part</u> are recorded as follows:[2]

---

[1]. Star of the Republic Museum, *Ring-Tailed Panthers and Cornstalk Lawyers*, (Washington, TX).

[2]. H.P.N. Gammel, *The Laws of Texas, 1822-1897, Volume 1, Journals of The Convention of the Free, Sovereign and Independent People of Texas, in General Convention Assembled*, The Gammel Book Company, 1898, Austin, TX, pp 823- 900.

Tuesday, March 1, 1836

There being a quorum of the delegates present, the Convention at Washington on the Brazos began, Tuesday, March 1, 1836. On motion of Mr. Everett, Mr. Collinsworth was called to the chair.

From the Municipality of Brazoria, delegates were recognized: Edwin Waller, James Collinsworth, and John S. D. Byrom.

Resolved, That the Convention proceed to the election of a President of their body. The question being taken it was agreed to. Mr. Everett nominated Richard Ellis[1] and there being no opposition, Mr. Ellis was declared unanimously elected President of the Convention, who was conducted to the chair by Messrs. Collinsworth and Everett.

On motion of Mr. Collinsworth, the Convention proceeded to the election of a Secretary to their body. Mr. Collinsworth nominated Mr. W. A. Farris.

On motion of Mr. Gazley, *Resolved*, That the President appoint a committee of five, to draft rules for the order and government of the Convention, And the question being taken thereon, it was decided in the affirmative: whereupon the President appointed Messrs. Gazley , Houston, Potter, Collinsworth and Everett, said committee.

---

[1]. Richard Ellis (1781–1846) was born in the "Tidewater Section" of Virginia. He studied law with the Richmond firm of Wirt and Wickham until 1806, when he was admitted to the Virginia bar and joined that law firm. Sometime between 1813 and 1817 Ellis left Virginia and settled at Huntsville, Madison County, and later at Tuscumbia, Franklin County, Alabama, where he established a plantation and continued the practice of law. Then, in 1818, he was elected one of two delegates to represent Franklin County at the Alabama Constitutional Convention.

In February 22, 1834 Ellis moved his family and more than twenty-five slaves to Pecan Point in the disputed territory claimed by Mexico as part of Old Red River County and by the United States as part of Miller County, Arkansas. Near the end of January, 1836 he was selected as one of five delegates to constitutional convention.

As the convention opened Ellis was unanimously elected president. On March 2, 1836, he signed the Texas Declaration of Independence as president of the convention. Although some observers were critical of him as a presiding officer, the general verdict is that he had a good grasp of parliamentary procedure and that he presided with a remarkable degree of gentleness and urbanity. Most importantly, he held the convention together for the seventeen days needed to draft a constitution for the Republic of Texas. [http://www.tshaonline.org/handbook/online/articles/fel16 Accessed 3/15/2011]

Chapter 6: Birth of the Republic of Texas

Wednesday, March 2, 1836

On motion of Mr. Collinsworth, *Resolved*, That Mr. Willis A. Farris be allowed to take a seat at the Secretary's table, to note and report the proceedings of the Convention, and the question being taken thereon, it was decided in the affirmative.

On motion of Mr. Collinsworth, the Convention resolved itself into a committee of the whole upon the report of the committee on the Declaration of Independence, Mr. Collinsworth in the chair. And after some time spent therein, on motion of Mr. Houston, the committee rose, and Mr. Collinsworth reported that the committee of the whole had under consideration the report of the committee on the Declaration of Independence, and had instructed him to report the same with the following caption: *The unanimous Declaration of Independence made by the Delegates of the People of Texas, in General Convention at the town of Washington, on the 2nd day of March, 1836.*

Thursday, March 3, 1836

On March 3, 1836, fifty-two delegates signed a Declaration of Independence from Mexico. On motion of Mr. Hardeman, Messrs. Houston, Collinsworth, and Thomas were added to the committee appointed to draft a constitution.

On motion of Mr. Collinsworth, *Resolved*: That the papers and documents transferred to the convention be referred to a committee of five delegates for examination and report. And the question being taken thereon, it was decided in the affirmative; whereupon the President appointed Messrs. Collinsworth, Gazley, Hamilton, Childress, and Goodrich said committee.

Friday, March 4, 1836

On motion of Mr. Collinsworth, the following Preamble and resolution were introduced: Whereas we are now in a state of Revolution, and threatened by a large invading army, from the central government of Mexico; and whereas our present situation, and the emergency of the present crisis, renders it indispensably necessary that we should have an army in the

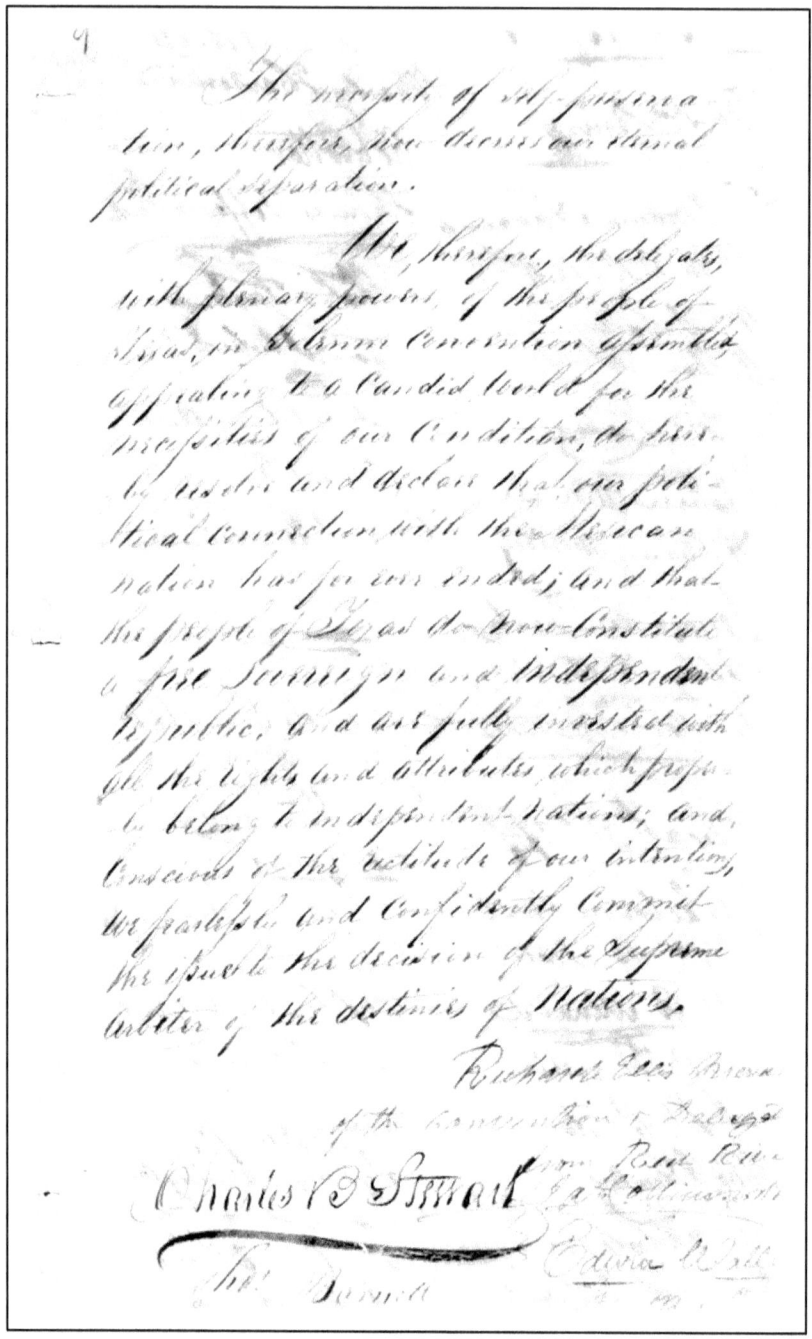

The first signature page of the Texas Declaration of Independence

field; and, whereas, it is also necessary that there should be one Supreme head or Commander in Chief, and due degrees of subordination defined, established and strictly observed, Therefore, be it *Resolved*, that General Samuel Houston be appointed Commander in Chief of all the land forces of the Texian Army, both regulars, volunteers and militia, while in actual service, and endowed with all the rights, privileges and powers due to a Commander in Chief in the United States of America, and that he forthwith proceed to take command, establish headquarters and organize the army accordingly. On motion of Mr. Collinsworth, *Resolved*, that the rule requiring the resolution to lay one day on the table, be dispensed with, and that the Resolution be forthwith put upon its passage.

Sunday, March 6, 1836

Colonel W. Barrett Travis' letter of February 24 from the Alamo was read:

Commandancy of the Alamo – Bejar,
Feby. 24th, 1836 –

To the people of Texas & all Americans in the world –
Fellow citizens & compatriots –

    I am besieged, by a thousand or more of the Mexicans under Santa Anna – I have sustained a continual Bombardment & cannonade for 24 hours & have not lost a man – The enemy has demanded a surrender at discretion, otherwise, the garrison are to be put to the sword, if the fort is taken – I have answered the demand with a cannon shot, & our flag still waves proudly from the walls – I shall never surrender or retreat.
    Then, I call on you in the name of Liberty, of patriotism & everything dear to the American character, to come to our aid, with all dispatch – The enemy is receiving reinforcements daily & will no doubt increase to three or four thousand in four or five days. If this call is neglected, I am determined to sustain myself as long as possible & die like a soldier who never forgets what is due to his own honor & that of his country – VICTORY OR DEATH.

William Barret Travis
Lt. Col. comdt.

P.S. The Lord is on our side – When the enemy appeared in sight we had not three bushels of corn – We have since found in deserted houses 80 or 90 bushels and got into the walls 20 or 30 head of Beeves – Travis

After hearing this, Messrs. Collinsworth, Childress, and Rusk opposed the adoption of a resolution introduced by Mr. Potter to adjourn. "On motion of Mr. Thomas, *Resolved*, That a standing military committee, consisting of five members, be appointed by the President. And the question being taken thereon, it was decided in the affirmative; whereupon the President appointed Messrs. Collinsworth, Rusk, Power, Gaines, and Fisher of Gonzales, said committee.

However, some of the convention members left prior to conclusion, others quickly dispersed after the meeting to join efforts for the defense of Texas and to aid the flight of refugees on the Runaway Scrape[1] in front of Santa Anna's army. Without waiting for the delegates to vote on his recommendation General Houston hurried from the hall to prepare for his early departure. He was delayed more than an hour waiting for his commission, for which Chairman Collinsworth's resolution, indorsed by President Ellis, had to serve. Then, on that memorable Sunday, March 6, 1836, when the state of affairs at the Alamo was as yet unknown, along with his Inspector General, an aide-de-camp and a courier, Houston set out on the 115-mile ride west to Gonzales.[2]

In fact, the final assault and capture was under way as the representatives were hearing Travis's letter read. Before daybreak on the morning of March 6, 1836, columns of Mexican soldiers emerged from the predawn darkness and headed for the Alamo's walls. Cannon and small arms fire from inside

---

[1]. The term "Runaway Scrape" was the name Texans applied to the flight from their homes when Antonio López de Santa Anna began his attempted conquest of Texas in February 1836. When Sam Houston arrived in Gonzales on March 11 and was informed of the fall of the Alamo, he decided to retreat to the Colorado River and ordered all inhabitants to accompany him. Couriers were dispatched from Gonzales to carry the news of the fall of the Alamo, and when they received that news, people all over Texas began to leave everything and make their way to safety.

Houston's retreat marked the beginning of the Runaway Scrape on a really large scale. Washington-on-the-Brazos was deserted by March 17, and about April 1 Richmond was evacuated, as were the settlements on both sides of the Brazos River. The further retreat of Houston toward the Sabine left all of the settlements between the Colorado and the Brazos unprotected, and the settlers in that area at once began making their way toward Louisiana or Galveston Island. Many persons died and were buried where they fell. The flight continued until news came of the victory in the battle of San Jacinto. [Carolyn Callaway Covington, "RUNAWAY SCRAPE," *Handbook of Texas Online* http://www.tshaonline.org/handbook/online/articles/pfr01, accessed March 06, 2011.]

[2]. M. K. Wisehart, *American Giant*, (Washington: Robert B. Luce, Inc., 1962.

the Alamo beat back several attacks. Regrouping, the Mexicans scaled the walls and rushed into the compound. Once inside, they turned a captured cannon on the Long Barrack and church, blasting open the barricaded doors. The desperate struggle continued until the defenders were overwhelmed. By sunrise, the battle had ended and Santa Anna entered the Alamo compound to survey the scene of his victory.[1] The defenders held out for 13 days against Santa Anna's army.

Monday, March 7, 1836

On motion of Mr. Collinsworth, Messrs. Thomas, Smith, and Menard were added to the Committee on Military Affairs. Collinsworth was elected chairman.

The same day James received a letter from Sam Houston:

Doctor Hoxies', March 7th, 1836

Dear Sir,
   Before I proceed on my way this morning, you will allow me to call your attention, if you please, with that of the committee, to the subject of fortifying "Live Oak Point," on the bay of Copano. Troops coming from the U. States via New Orleans can sail for that point on armed vessels with artillery and lumber sufficient for such fortifications as will be necessary for the present. The cannon there placed should be large pieces, 12s and 18s, and very few will suffice. Col. Power can give you all the information that you may desire; I will only suggest that it will give us command of all the supplies destined for Goliad and San Antonio, if the enemy should even possess them. If a liberal appropriation of money should be made for the army, although we should not immediately receive it, it will keep down much discontent until it can be had.
   I pray you to have the Cherokee treaty ratified, and Major Washington Lewis, residing at Masters' on the road, appointed agent for the Cherokees to reside near Bowls'. This will be of importance to the safety of the frontier. If any plan be devised by which the Comanches can be approached by the head waters of the Brazos, and they induced to fall down and range upon the Laredo route to Bexar and steal horses, it will be important. A Mr. Dillard, residing at the Falls of the Brazos will be a proper person to communicate with. Measures should be attended to if possible to prevent the Creek Indians from emigrating to the East of Texas. Col. Rusk can inform you of the fact of A. Hotchkiss' interest in inducing the Indians to migrate to the country.

---

[1]. http://www.thealamo.org/battle/battle.php Accessed 3/6/2011

The evidence is conclusive. It would be well if the steam packet "Wm Brown," if purchased, should have such guns placed on her as would enable her to throw grape and canister into the enemy in close contact, as I am told she cannot carry large pieces. If Copano is occupied by us, the enemy will never advance into the colonies.

God bless you—and may you long continue useful to Texas. I rode until late last night, and rose early this morning. Major Hockley desires to be remembered to you. Please salute my friends who ask for me.

Ever yours truly,
(signed) Sam. Houston.

There is a Mr. Blount in Washington, who deserves a Captaincy in the cavalry, if you should think proper to advance him. I pray that all appointments in the army, since the 6th of January, made by the self-styled "Council," may be set aside, if the persons should be afterwards appointed. Please see Doctor Everitt, and he can speak to you of a Mr Blount of Jasper. He only received a Lieutenacy when he should have been advanced.

Yours truly,
(signed) Houston.

What say you of a resolution that Texas is a part of Louisiana, and the U. States by treaty of 1803?

[To]
Hon. James Collinsworth.
Chairman M[ilitary]. Committee.

Tuesday, March 8, 1836

On motion of Mr. Hardeman, *Resolved,* That all subjects not directly connected with the constitution of this republic, lay on the table until that instrument be adopted by this convention. Which, on motion of Mr. Collinsworth, was laid on the table.

Mr. Collinsworth, chairman of the committee on public documents, made the following report:

In regard to the loan contracted by your commissioners in the United States, your committee are [sic] of opinion that it is not so advantageous to this government as could have been desired. But when it is considered that the late consultation had declared for the republican principles of the constitution of eighteen hundred and twenty-four, which gave us no distinct national existence; which declaration, however proper at the time, tended very much to abate the enthusiasm felt in our behalf. And

Chapter 6: Birth of the Republic of Texas

when it is further considered, that this fact alone rendered any security on Texas extremely precarious, and that too, at a time when our national existence depended upon the immediate reception of money, provisions and arms, to carry on the war, your committee are satisfied that the loans submitted were the best that could have been made under the circumstances. Add to this the great importance of at all times preserving good faith as a nation, your committee are of opinion that it is due to your commissioners, and to yourselves, that the loans should be unhesitatingly ratified. Your committee having also had under consideration the treaty made by your late commissioners, with the small tribes of Indians specified in said treaty, are of opinion that said treaty is probably as favorable as could have been made at the time under all the circumstances, and recommends its ratification. They have also had under consideration the proposition of John T. Lamar, which proposition is herewith submitted as part of this report, and recommended its adoption.

Jas. Collinsworth, Chairman.

Thursday, March 10, 1836

On motion of Mr. Collinsworth, the convention took up the report of the committee of the whole upon the constitution.

Mr. Collinsworth, chairman of the committee on military affairs, made the following report; to wit: Convention Hall, March 12, 1836. To Captain Joseph L. Bennett.- Sir, -You will proceed immediately to the head quarters of the commander-in-chief, and report yourself to him: upon which, and being mustered into service, he will forward to the proper authority the necessary certificate and commissions for yourself and inferior company officers will be regularly issued. On your way to head quarters, you will be authorized to purchase, on the credit of the government, such provisions as may be necessary for the use of your company, enjoining on you strict economy. And when you cannot otherwise obtain provisions, you are authorized to press such as may be absolutely necessary: but in doing this, you will act with the greatest forbearance, and in such manner as to avoid, as far as possible, all individual distress: and should it be necessary for you to kill any stock, you will keep an account of the marks and brands, so that their proper owners may be compensated: and when you purchase provisions on the faith of the government, you will give the owners certificates thereof. Jas. Collinsworth, Chairman of committee on military affairs.

Mr. Collinsworth submitted sundry public documents from Messrs. McKinney & Williams, which were on motion referred to the committee on finance.

Mr. Rusk introduced the following resolutions: *Resolved* that a standing Committee on the state of the Republic be appointed by the President: which was laid on the table, under rule, till tomorrow. *Resolved* that a Committee of five be appointed as a standing Committee of finance; which was accepted. Whereupon the president appointed Messrs. Collinsworth, Gazley, Hamilton, Childress, and Goodrich.

On motion of Mr. Rusk, *Resolved* that a committee of three be immediately appointed to draw copies of the late act organizing the militia and that the President of this body issue his orders under the provisions of that act ordering out one third of the militia: which was adopted; and thereupon the President appointed Messrs. Carson, Collinsworth, and Childress said committee.

Sunday, March 13, 1836

By March 13, 1836, Houston, still at Gonzales, had lost the whereabouts of Fannin, who had been forced by a wagon breakdown to give up his march to the Alamo. To Military Affairs Chairman James Collinsworth, Houston stressed "the great importance of ... the defense of Matagorda and Lavaca Bays," and reported more Texas losses resulting from broken supply lines and multiple commands: "The projected expedition to Matamoras ... has already cost us over two hundred and thirty-seven lives ... Colonel Johnson's men have been murdered.[1]

Tuesday, March 15, 1836

A letter from Genl. Sam Houston [to Fannin], announcing the fall of the Alamo, was read by the President:

To Col. Fannin, Commanding at Goliad

Sir:

On my arrival here [Gonzales] this afternoon the following intelligence was received through a Mexican, supposed to be friendly, though his account has been contradicted in some parts by another, who arrived with him. It is therefore only given to you as a rumor though I fear a melancholy portion of it will be found true.

Anselmo Borgara states that he left the Alamo on Sunday the 6th inst. and is six days from Arroche's ranch; that the Alamo was attacked on Sunday morning at the dawn of day, by about two thousand three hundred men, and carried a short time before sunrise by a loss of five hundred and twenty-one Mexicans killed and as many wounded. Col. Travis had only one hundred and fifty effective men, out of his entire force of one hundred and eighty-seven. After the fort was carried seven men surrendered, and called for Santa Anna, and for quarter. They were murdered by his order. Col. Bowie was sick in bed and was also

---

[1]. Sue Flanagan, *Sam Houston's Texas*, (Meriden, CT: Meriden Gravure Company, 1964), p 22.

murdered. The enemy expect a reinforcement of fifteen hundred men under Gen. Cordelle, and a reserve of fifteen hundred to follow them. He also informs us that Ugartechea had arrived with two millions of specie for the payment of the troops.

The bodies of the Americans were burned after the massacre. Alternate layers of wood and bodies were laid together and set on fire. Lieut. Dickinson, who had a wife and child in the fort, after having fought with desperate courage tied his child to his back and leaped from the top of a two-story building. Both were killed by the fall. I have little doubt but that the Alamo has fallen whether the above particulars are all true may be questionable. You are therefore referred to the enclosed order.

P.S. In confirmation of the truth of the fall of the Alamo, I have ascertained that Col. Travis intended firing signal guns at three different periods each day until succor should arrive. No signal guns have been heard since Sunday, though a scouting party have just returned who approached within twelve miles of it, and remained there forty-eight hours.

After declaring their independence and knowing that a vast army under Antonio Lopez de Santa Anna was advancing to restore Mexican sovereignty in Texas and crush the rebellion, these brave individuals remained at Washington to write a constitution, establish a government, and elect officials. On March 15, news of the fall of the Alamo "spread like fire in high grass" and caused "complete panic." According to signer James Collinsworth, upon hearing the news Convention President Richard Ellis rose in his seat, pulled a small pistol from his pocket, and proposed adjourning to Bradshaw's near the Neches River as "the enemy would be upon us before morning." Cooler heads prevailed and the delegates remained, but the next day signer Charles Stewart noted: "our situation is very bad today we finish the Constitution hurry through the rest of the business, and prepare for desperate efforts.[1]

---

[1]. Star of the Republic Museum, *Ring-Tailed Panthers and Cornstalk Lawyers*, (Washington, TX).

Wednesday, March 16, 1836

Mr. Collinsworth, Chairman of the Committee of Finance, submitted a report as to the claims of Messrs. McKinney & Williams against the Government, which was laid on the table.

Mr. Collinsworth, Chairman of the Committee on Military Affairs asked leave for said committee to be discharged, which was done.

At midnight on March 16, a Constitution was adopted followed by an ordinance organizing a provisional government.[1]

Thursday, March 17, 1836

David Burnet[2] was elected Ad interim president of the new Republic on March 17, 1836. His cabinet members were Vice-President: Lorenzo de Zavala, Secretary of State: Samuel Price Carson, Secretary of War: Thomas J. Rusk, Secretary of Treasury: Bailey Hardeman and Attorney General: David Thomas.

Retreat!

When Houston had retreated from Gonzales to the Colorado on March 17, 1836, he at once wrote another letter to Mr. Collinsworth in which he reported that he had with him about 600 men, including the rear guards which he had sent back to accompany families making their way eastward.[3]

---

[1]. Star of the Republic Museum, *Ring-Tailed Panthers and Cornstalk Lawyers*, (Washington, TX).

[2]. David G. Burnet, (1788–1870) was born in Newark, New Jersey, was orphaned at an early age and raised by his older half brothers. All of his life he strove to achieve the prominence of his father and brothers. Burnet lived with his brothers in Cincinnati, studied law in his brother Jacob's office, and followed the same conservative politics.

Burnet was against independence for Texas in 1835, although he deplored the tendency of the national government toward a dictatorship. Thus his more radical neighbors did not choose him as a delegate to either the Consultation or the Convention of 1836. His ad interim presidency of the Republic of Texas lasted from March 17 to October 22, 1836, and was very difficult. His actions angered Sam Houston, the army, the vice president, many cabinet members, and the public, and he left office embittered, intending never to return home, where a number of neighbors had turned against him. In 1838 he entered the race for vice president and rode Mirabeau B. Lamar's coattails to victory.
[(http://www.tshaonline.org/handbook/online/articles/fbu46), accessed March 25, 2011.]

[3]. Sam Houston Dixon and Louis Wiltz Kemp, *The Heroes of San Jacinto*, (Houston: The Anson Jones Press, 1932), p 6.

Chapter 6: Birth of the Republic of Texas

They camped near present Columbus on March 20, recruiting and reinforcements having increased its size to 1,200 men. Houston's scouts reported Mexican troops west of the Colorado to number 1,325. On March 25 the Texans learned of James W. Fannin's defeat at Goliad and many of the men left the army to join their families on the "Runaway Scrape."[1]

Houston then led his troops to San Felipe de Austin by March 28 and by March 30 to the Jared E. Groce plantation on the Brazos River, where they camped and drilled for a fortnight.

Ad interim President David G. Burnet ordered Houston to stop his retreat; Secretary of War Thomas J. Rusk[2] urged him to take a

M.K.Wisehart, *American Giant*, p 185.

---

[1]. Walter Prescott Webb, Editor-In-Chief, *Handbook of Texas, Vol 1*, (Austin: Texas State Historical Association, 1952), p 377.

[2]. Thomas Jefferson Rusk (1803–1857) was born in Pendleton District, South Carolina, son of an Irish stonemason immigrant. The family rented land from John C. Calhoun, who helped Rusk secure a position in the office of the Pendleton County district clerk, where he could earn a living while studying law. After admission to the bar in 1825, Rusk began his law practice in Clarksville, Georgia.

He lived in the gold region of Georgia and made sizable mining investments. In 1834, however, the managers of the company in which he had invested embezzled all the funds and fled to Texas. Rusk pursued them to Nacogdoches but never recovered the money.

As a delegate from Nacogdoches to the Convention of 1836, Rusk not only signed the Texas Declaration of Independence but also chaired the committee to revise the constitution. The ad interim government, installed on March 17, 1836, appointed Rusk Secretary of War.

more decisive course.

On April 6, 1836, James was made aide-de-camp by General Houston with the rank of Major.[1] His role was described in the following letter from Rusk to Williamson:[2]

Army Orders
Head Quarters
Camp West of Brazos
7th April 1836

To Major R. M. Williamson

Sir
You are ordered forthwith to report yourself at Head Quarters. My aid de camp, Major Jas. Collinsworth, will assume command at Washington and the control of the men and troops at that point. He has my orders to keep out spies and to adopt such measures as he may see proper for the safety of the place.

I disapprove the killing of those two Mexicans - they should have been sent to me for examination. I have no idea but that they were deserters from the enemy and important information might have been obtained from them.

I order without exception the destruction of all ardent spirits at Washington and wherever it may be found. I have not delegated any power to any person or persons to arrest & try persons for offences. The discretionary powers given to Maj. Collinsworth are the first issued by me. I wish Col. Pettus to repair to camp and report to me. Major Collinsworth has power to call all persons into service, and to act to his discretion, saving life.

By order of T. J. Rusk, Secy of War and

When informed that the Alamo had fallen and the Mexicans were moving eastward, Rusk helped President Burnet to move the government to Harrisburg. Rusk ordered all the coastal communities to organize militias.

From May 4 to October 31, 1836, he served as commander in chief of the Army of the Republic of Texas, with the rank of brigadier general. He followed the Mexican troops westward as they retired from Texas to be certain of their retreat beyond the Rio Grande.
[http://www.tshaonline.org/handbook/online/articles/fru16, Accessed 3/15/2011]

[1]. Sam Houston Dixon and Louis Wiltz Kemp, *The Heroes of San Jacinto*, (Houston: The Anson Jones Press, 1932), p 45.

[2]. Jenkins, *Papers of the Texas Revolution,* Volume 5, p. 362.

Chapter 6: Birth of the Republic of Texas

Sam Houston, Comdr in Chief

After the hasty adjournment of the Convention on the 17th, Collinsworth repaired to the army. On April 8, 1836, at Washington, he wrote General Houston:[1]

Sir

In compliance with your order I have attempted to organize the force at this place subject to duty. When I arrived Maj. Williamson had but few men enrolled for duty. I have now almost an entire company of Volunteers who performed their duty with great alacrity and good order. Things here now in great confusion, many families of all classes are camped in the bottoms on the east side of the Brazos and in a most deplorable condition. Men women and children subject to all the inconveniences of the dampness of a low bottom much overflowed & without medical attention. Under these circumstances I have appointed Dr. B. B. Goodrich Surgeon at this post until further ordered by yourself. Pettis has left in search of some deserters before I arrived at this Post & have not returned. I have thus far continued Maj. Williamson with me because my want of information in regard to this part of the country rendered it necessary.

I crossed the river yesterday and finding the bottom a scene of drunkenness & debauchery, when ladies of proud claims to decency and respectability were insulted in my presence, in compliance with your order I destroyed without reserve all the spirits I could find to which altho' there was no actual resistance but many murmurs & threats. I was more than rewarded for these in hearing the prayers of a venerable matron sent up to heaven in my behalf for the act, without being conscious that I was in hearing. I think there will be good order here among those we may be enable to embody. The militia law is defective in requiring the persons subject to duty to be notified; after notice is given it should be their duty to enroll themselves.

In conclusion I have to say we have no information of the enemy having been nearer than Bastrop on the West side of the Colorado. I hope I shall be discharged from this place as soon as possible as I have performed all the duty contemplated. The troops here conduct themselves with the most perfect good order.
                                            James Collinsworth

A few days later James prepared a memo[1] retained as a debit to the firm supplying the spirits:

---

[1]. Louis Wiltz Kemp, *The Signers of the Texas Declaration of Independence*, (Salado Texas: The Anson Jones Press, 1959), pp 80-81.

The Government of the Republic of Texas

April 10, 1836

To Martin Clow & Company
55 gal whiskey   @/2.00 $110.00
35 gal brandy   @/4.00 $140.00
                                        $250.00
The above spirits were destroyed by order of Saml. Houston Commander in Chief by

        James Collinsworth
        Aid de Camp

---

[1]. Republic Claims, *Texas State Library and Archives Commission, Archives &Manuscripts,* Reel 253, Image 619.
[http://www.tsl.state.tx.us/arc/repclaims/viewdetails.php?id=22367 Accessed 3/12/2011]

Remarks concerning the proceedings of the Constitutional Convention made sometime later by James Collinsworth to Mirabeau Lamar:[1]

A convention of the people of Texas met at Washington the first day of March 1836. When I arrived it seemed to be understood that Richard Ellis from that part of Red River under the Conventional Jurisdiction of the U. States was to be President.

He was accordingly nominated to that station without opposition.

And the very first acts done by him in the appointment of his committees he clearly exhibited the course he subsequently intended to pursue. He united himself with Robert Potter of famous memory and other avarious [sic] land speculators who in order to carry their own speculations where they had pretended to purchase & had actually procured conveyances to head many of [them] had never been bona fide settled : Attempted to pass the famous agrarian law declaring all grants of land for [more] than one league of land absolutely void. This measure was warmly opposed by myself in the Judiciary Committee in a speech which I shall shortly lay before the world. The committee voted down the proposition by a small majority. But Mr. Childress, who together with Ellis, Hamilton, Robertson & others were deeply interested in defeating these claims, modified the measure so as to make all grants for more than eleven leagues void and all eleven league claims not located in strict conformity with law void as to their location.

During the short space of ___ days the present Constitution was formed and the late government ad interim organized. You know all about that . . . All the candidates nominated for atty gen'l offered to name their claims in my favor if I would accept, which I declined upon the ground that a battle decisive of the existence of the Country was obliged soon to [be] fought. As I then stated, when the lives of my friends & the existence my Country was to be periled, I chose to be with them.

I shall never forget the alarm manifested by many honorable members of the Convention the night the news arrived of the fall of the Alamo. The venerable President of that body rose in his seat with much trepidation and pulling a small pistol from his pocket proposed adjourning to Bradshaws, as the enemy would be upon us before morning. This was objected to & overruled. But the news of the fall of the Alamo was unpleasing music to the ears of these aforesaid land speculators and they were willing to lead the retreat & abandon for a time their unhallowed speculations. And when now [sic] they when the souls of men were tried.

---

[1]. Louis Wiltz Kemp, *The Signers of the Texas Declaration of Independence*, (Salado Texas: The Anson Jones Press, 1959), pp 78-80.

> The Commander in Chief was also appointed by the Convention and, as Chairman of the Committee on military affairs, I reported a resolution appointing Sam Houston.
> This met with but little opposition except from Robert Potter who opposed it in a long & animated speech in which he urged many objections. (I wish you could [see] Farris notes & journals as it would throw much light on this subject.) My return to Brazoria and subsequently rejoining the army and all the subsequent operations are as well known to yourself as to me all of which you saw & part of which you
> . . .
> My health from the time I came to the Country had precluded me from taking any part in the proceedings that led to, and what was done in the Consultation, hence you will be enabled to get better information from others.

Although news of the military action in Texas was spreading all across the United States, James' brother, John, could not have known any details of the events of the same date of his letter written from Wisconsin on April 8 to their sister Parmelia Ann Collinsworth Davis:

> *Fort Winnebago [Wisconsin]*
> *8 April 1836*
>
> Dear Sister
> Your kind favor of the 8th was received yesterday and with pleasure I hasten to answer it by the mail which departs tomorrow. I cannot express my feelings at this moment. You have told me many things which I did not know before. I am glad that you have recovered from your sickness and that a bountiful Providence may continue to watch over and protect you and yours, my dear sister, is my most earnest wish and constant prayer. I hope the time may yet come when we shall be all united and happy.
> Dear Sister before I open my heart in full to you I will proceed to inform you of all I know about James, George and my own affairs. James is in Texas. I have several letters from him within two or three month past in which he informs me that he has made up his mind to remain in Texas his life. He has urged me very strongly to resign my commission in the Army and go there also. From the prospects he holds out and from the information I have had from other source, I have determined to do so. I have resigned and as soon as I hear that the President of the United States [Jackson] has accepted my resignation I will depart for Texas. This will probably be about the 20th of next month [May].
> James informs me that there will, in all probability, be an independent government established in Texas and that he expects to be a prominent member of it and that I shall have an excellent opportunity of gaining wealth and fame and he says that he has but little doubt that he

will make a fortune in a short time. All this, I fear, will not be attained without a struggle with the Mexicans and perhaps with the Indians. This, however, I hope will not be long and then I trust we shall all be happy and united.

I have not heard a word of [brother] George since last I saw you, neither can I imagine where he is. The last I heard from him was when I was in Tennessee a little more than a year since. James told me that one of the Robertsons [their brother Benjamin Franklin Collinsworth's wife's family] had told him that he [Robertson] had seen George in the fall previous [1834] on his way to New Orleans from which I had always supposed until received the last letter from James that he was in Texas. But he cannot be there as I suppose James would have informed me of it.

As to the Collinsworth who was killed in Texas by the Indians, I expect the person is David Collinsworth, our cousin, a brother to our cousin George. They were both in Texas fighting in the Texan army. George was a Captain and David, a lieutenant. James informs me and I also saw it in the papers that David was killed last fall, it was supposed, by some Indians. I have not heard that any George Collinsworth has been killed. And I do not think any has as I would have heard of it. The last time I heard of George M. Collinsworth, our cousin, he was still in Texas, a Captain of Cavalry.

Most truly your friend and affectionate brother

J. T. Collinsworth[1]

---

[1]. Transcription of a letter received from Caroline Davis Tate of Houston TX, a descendant of James' sister, Parmelia.

Chapter 7 - The Battle of San Jacinto

The Texas A&M University[1] web site is the source for the following description and map of the Battle of San Jacinto, except as noted.

Because Houston had shown no disposition to fight so far, Santa Anna decided to take possession of the coast and seaports, as a step in his plan to round up the revolutionists. Crossing the Brazos at Fort Bend (now called Richmond) on the 11th, the Mexican general proceeded on April 14 on the road to Harrisburg, taking with him about 700 men and one twelve-pounder cannon.

Apparently not known by Santa Anna at this time was the capture on April 3, 1836 of the U.S. merchant marine ship *Pocket* with its contraband arms and supplies. These provisions of food and gunpowder were ultimately assigned to Houston's army. The event was noted in an April 12 letter from President Burnet to James Collinsworth:

A prize has been brought to Galveston by Captain [Jeremiah] Brown. The government has passed a decree to establish the district court. . . . We want an able judge in the district where the trial must take place. Will you then accept the office of district judge for the district of Brazoria?[2]

James declined David G. Burnet's appointment, apparently keeping himself available for a higher office.

Santa Anna arrived at Harrisburg on April 15 where he learned that the Burnet government had gone down Buffalo Bayou to New Washington, about 18 miles southeast. After burning Harrisburg, Santa Anna sped after them. On the 19th when he arrived at New Washington he learned that the new Texas government had fled to Galveston. Santa Anna then set out for that area.

Meanwhile, on April 11th, the Texans at Groce's received two cannon, known to history as the *"Twin Sisters,"* a gift from citizens of Cincinnati, Ohio. Thus fortified, General Houston, after a consultation with Rusk, decided to move on to the east side of the Brazos. The river being very high, the steamboat *Yellow Stone* and a yawl were used to ferry the army, horses, cattle and baggage across. The movement began on the 12th and was completed at 1 p.m. on the 13th.

Many of his officers and men, as well as government officials, believed that Houston's strategy was to lead the pursuing Mexicans to the Sabine River, the eastern border of Texas. There, it was known, were camped

---

[1]. http://www.tamu.edu/faculty/ccbn/dewitt/batsanjacinto.htm Accessed 3/7/2011

[2]. George P. Garrison, *Texas Historical Quarterly, Volume 12, No. 4, April 1909*, C. T. Neu, *The Case of the Brig Pocket*, Texas State Historical Association, p 282.

United States troops under General Pendelton Gaines, with whose help the Texans might turn on their foes and destroy them. However, on April 17, when Roberts' place was reached, Houston took the Harrisburg road instead of the one toward the Louisiana line, much to the gratification of his men. On April 18 the army marched twenty miles to White Oak Bayou in the Heights District of the present city of Houston.

From two prisoners, captured by Erasmus "Deaf" Smith, the famous Texas spy, Houston first learned that the Mexicans had burned Harrisburg and had gone down the west side of the bayou and of San Jacinto River, and that Santa Anna in person was in command. In his march downstream Santa Anna had been forced to cross the bridge over Vince's Bayou, a tributary of Buffalo Bayou, which was out of its banks. He would have to cross the same bridge to return. Viewing this strategic situation on the morning of the 19th, Houston told his troops it looked as if they would soon get action.

Houston took a brief moment that morning to write the note below to his friend, Col. Henry Raguet in Nacogdoches. A deep friendship existed between Sam Houston and the Raguet family. An interesting incident had occurred a few weeks before the battle of San Jacinto. Houston was a guest at Colonel Raguet's home, in Nacogdoches, and while sitting with his back toward the front door of the house and talking with Anna Raguet, who later became Mrs. Anna Irion, and Colonel Raguet, his host, he was approached from behind by a Mexican, who suddenly slipped in at the open door and who, with upraised dagger, attempted to assassinate Houston, but he was frustrated in the attempt by Anna Raguet, who sprang at the Mexican and seized the knife, thereby saving the life of the famous general.[1]

Camp at Harrisburg, 19th April, 1836.[2]

To Col. H[enry] Raguet, Nacogdoches, Texas:

This morning we are in preparation to meet Santa Anna. It is the only chance of saving Texas. From time to time I have looked for reinforcements in vain. The convention adjourning to Harrisburg struck panic throughout the country. Texas could have started at least 4,000 men; we only have about 700 to march with besides the camp guard. We go to conquer. It is wisdom growing out of necessity to meet and fight the enemy now. Every consideration enforces it. No previous occasion would justify it. The troops are in fine spirits, and now is the time for action.

---

[1]. Francis White Johnson, *A History of Texas and Texans, Vol. 4*, (Chicago and New York: The American Historical Society, 1914), p 1820.

[2]. Telegraph and Texas Register, (Houston, TX), Vol. 2, No. 20, Ed. 1, Saturday, June 3, 1837.

Adj't Gen'l Wharton, Ins. Gen. Hockley, Aid-de-camp Horton, aids-de-camp W. H. Patton, Collinsworth, Volunteer aids Perry, Perry, Maj. Cook, assistant insp. gen. will be with me.

We will use our best efforts to fight the enemy, to such advantage as will insure victory, though the odds is greatly against us. I leave the result in the hands of a wise God, and rely upon his providence. My country will do justice to those who serve her. The rights for which we fight will be secured, and Texas free.

SAM. HOUSTON, Com'r in chief.
Col. Rusk is in the field.

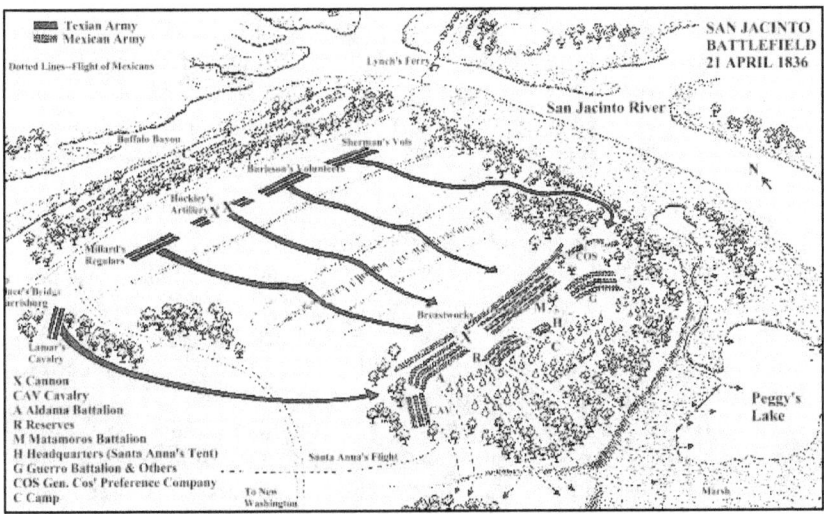

Houston's force crossed Buffalo Bayou to the west side on the evening of the 19th. Some 248 men, mostly sick and non-effective, were left with the baggage at the camp opposite Harrisburg. The march was continued until midnight.

At dawn April 20 the Texans resumed their trek down the bayou to intercept the Mexicans. At Lynch's ferry, near the juncture of Buffalo Bayou and San Jacinto River, they captured a boat laden with supplies for Santa Anna. This probably was some of the plunder of Harrisburg or New Washington. Ascertaining that none of the enemy forces had crossed, the Texans drew back about a mile on the Harrisburg road, and encamped in a skirt of timber protected by a rising ground.

That afternoon, Colonel Sidney Sherman, with a small detachment of cavalry engaged the enemy infantry, almost bringing on a general action. In the clash two Texans were wounded and several horses were killed. In this preliminary skirmish Mirabeau B. Lamar, a private from Georgia, so distinguished himself that on the next day he was placed in command of the cavalry.

Santa Anna's blue-uniformed army made camp under the high ground overlooking a marsh, about three-fourths of a mile from the Texas camp. They threw up breastworks of trunks, baggage, pack-saddles and other equipment. Both sides prepared for the expected conflict.

The Texans awoke to find Thursday, April 21, a clear fine day. Refreshed by a breakfast of bread made with flour from the captured supplies and meat from beeves slaughtered the day before, they were eager to attack the enemy. They could see Santa Anna's flags floating over the enemy camp, and heard the Mexican bugle calls on the crisp morning air.

It was discovered at about nine o'clock that General Martín Perfecto de Cos, Santa Anna's brother-in-law, had crossed Vince's bridge, about eight miles behind the Texans' camp, with some 540 picked troops, swelling the enemy forces to about 1265. General Houston ordered "Deaf" Smith and a detail to destroy the bridge and prevent further enemy reinforcements. This also would prevent the retreat of either the Texans or the Mexicans toward Harrisburg. In dry weather Vince's Bayou was about fifty feet wide and ten feet deep, but the excessive April rains had made it several times wider and deeper.

Shortly before noon, General Houston held a council of war with Colonels Edward Burleson and Sidney Sherman, Lieutenant Colonels Henry Millard, Alexander Somervell and Joseph L. Bennett, and Major Lysander Wells. Two of the officers suggested attacking the enemy in his position, while the others favored awaiting Santa Anna's attack. Houston withheld his own views, but later, after having formed his plan of battle, submitted it to Secretary of War Rusk, who approved it.

General Houston disposed his forces in battle order at about 3:30 in the afternoon. Over on the Mexican side all was quiet; many of the foemen were enjoying their customary siesta. The Texans' movements were screened by the trees and the rising ground, and evidently Santa Anna had no lookouts posted. Big, shaggy and commanding in his mud-stained unmilitary garb, the chieftain rode his horse up and down the line. *"Now hold your fire, men,"* he warned in his deep voice, *"until you get the order!"*

At the command, *"Advance,"* the patriots, 910 strong, moved quickly out of the woods and over the rise, deploying. Bearded and ragged from forty days in the field, they were a fierce-looking band. But their long rifles were clean and well oiled. Only one company, Captain William Wood's *"Kentucky Rifles,"* originally recruited by Sidney Sherman, wore uniforms. The battle line was formed with *Edward Burleson's* regiment in the center; Sherman's on the left wing; the artillery, under George W. Hockley, on Burleson's right; the infantry, under Henry Millard, on the right of the artillery; and the cavalry, led by Lamar, on the extreme right.

Silently and tensely the Texas battle line swept across the prairie and swale that was No Man's land, the men bending low. As the troops advanced, "Deaf" Smith galloped up and told Houston, *"Vince's bridge has been cut down."* The General announced it to the men. Now both armies were cut off from retreat in all directions but one. With a roughly circular moat formed

Chapter 7: The Battle of San Jacinto

by Vince's and Buffalo Bayous to the west and north, San Jacinto River to the north and east, and by the marshes and the bay to the east and southeast, only a southwesterly direction is left.

At close range, the two little cannon, drawn by rawhide thongs, were wheeled into position and belched their charges of iron slugs into the enemy barricade. Then the whole line, led by Sherman's men, sprang forward on the run, yelling, *"Remember the Alamo!" "Remember Goliad!"* All together they opened fire, blazing away practically point-blank at the surprised and panic-stricken Mexicans. They stormed over the breastworks, seized the enemy's artillery, and joined in hand-to-hand combat, emptying their pistols, swinging their guns as clubs, slashing right and left with their knives. Mexicans fell by the scores under the impact of the savage assault.

General Manuel Fernández Castrillón, a brave Mexican, tried to rally the swarthy Latins, but he was killed and his men became crazed with fright. Many threw down their guns and ran; many wailed, *"Me no Alamo!" "Me no Goliad!"* But their pleas won no mercy. The enraged revolutionists reloaded and chased after the stampeding enemy, shooting them, stabbing them, clubbing them to death. From the moment of the first collision the battle was a slaughter, frightful to behold. The fugitives ran in wild terror over the prairie and into the boggy marshes, but the avengers of the Alamo and Goliad followed and slew them, or drove them into the waters to drown. Men and horses, dead and dying, in the morass in the rear and right of the Mexican camp, formed a bridge for the pursuing Texans. Blood reddened the water. General Houston tried to check the execution but the fury of his men was beyond restraint.

Some of the Mexican cavalry tried to escape over Vince's bridge, only to find that the bridge was gone. In desperation, some of the flying horsemen spurred their mounts down the steep bank; some dismounted and plunged into the swollen stream. The Texans came up and poured a deadly fire into the welter of Mexicans struggling with the flood. Escape was virtually impossible.

General Houston rode slowly from the field of victory, his ankle shattered by a rifle ball. At the foot of the oak where he had slept the previous night be fainted and slid from his horse into the arms of Major Hockley, his chief of staff.

As the crowning stroke of a glorious day, General Rusk presented to him as a prisoner the Mexican general Don Juan Almonte, who had surrendered formally with about 400 men. The casualties, according to Houston's official report, numbered 630 Mexicans killed, 208 wounded, and 730 taken prisoner. As against this heavy score, only nine Texans were killed or mortally wounded, and thirty wounded less seriously. Most of their injuries came from the first scattered Mexican volley when the attackers stormed their barricade. The Texans captured a large supply of muskets, pistols, sabers, mules, horses, provisions, clothing, tents and paraphernalia, and $12,000 in silver.

Several Texas officers had accompanied Second Lt. William W. Summers back to the Mexican campground with the wagon, including Captain Isaac Moreland, Major James Collinsworth and Colonel Robert Coleman. Colonel Almonte, the English-speaking Mexican officer, was allowed to "collect Santa Anna's private baggage, all of which was put on the wagon and taken to camp on the bayou about 11 o'clock on the night after the battle."[1]

Santa Anna had disappeared during the battle, and the next day General Houston ordered a thorough search of the surrounding territory for him. In the afternoon Sergeant J. A. Sylvester spotted a Mexican slipping through the woods toward Vince's Bayou. Sylvester and his comrades caught the fugitive trying to hide in the high grass. He wore a common soldier's apparel round jacket, blue cotton pantaloons, skin cap and soldier's shoes. They took the captive to camp, and on the way, Mexican prisoners recognized him and cried, **"El Presidente!"** Thus his identity was betrayed; it was indeed the dictator from below the Rio Grande.

He was brought to General Houston, who lay under the headquarters oak, nursing his wounded foot. The Mexican President pompously announced, *"I am General Antonio Lopez de Santa Anna, and a prisoner of war at your disposition."* General Houston, suffering with pain, received him coldly. He sent for young Moses Austin Bryan and Lorenzo de Zavala Jr. to act as interpreters. Santa Anna cringed with fright as the excited Texas soldiers pressed around him, fearing mob violence.

He pleaded for the treatment due a prisoner of war. *"You can afford to be generous,"* he whined; *"you have captured the Napoleon of the 'West." "What claim have you to mercy?"* Houston retorted, *"when you showed none at the Alamo or at Goliad?"* They talked for nearly two hours, using Bryan, de Zavala and Almonte as interpreters. In the end Santa Anna agreed to write an order commanding all Mexican troops to evacuate Texas.

On April 25, 1836 General Houston made his official report of the battle to President Burnet, carefully describing the troop movements, the strategy of timing the attack, the results of the eighteen-minute battle and "tribute of our grateful thanks from that Being who rules the destinies of nations, and has, in the time of greatest need, enabled us to arrest a powerful invader whilst devastating our country."[2]

Thus ended the revolution of 1836 with an eighteen-minute battle which established Texas as a free republic and opened the way for the United States to extend its boundaries to the Rio Grande on the southwest and to the

---

[1]. Stephen L. Moore, *Eighteen Minutes: The Battle of San Jacinto and the Texas Independence Campaign* (Dallas. Lanham. Boulder. New York. (Oxford: Republic of Texas Press), page 370.

[2]. William Kennedy, *Texas: The Rise, Progress, and Prospects of The Republic of Texas, VOL II, Second Edition*, (London: R. Hastings, 1841), pp 222-227.

Pacific on the west. Few military engagements in history have been more decisive or of more far-reaching ultimate influence than the battle of San Jacinto.

James made a brilliant record for bravery in this engagement. He was honorably mentioned by General Rusk in his official report of the Battle of San Jacinto to President Burnet. Of Mr. Collinsworth, Mr. Rusk said: "While I do justice to all in expressing my high admiration of the bravery and gallant conduct of our officers and men, I hope I may be indulged in the expression of my highest approbation of the chivalrous conduct of Major James Collinsworth in almost every part of the engagement."[1]

Soon after the battle James filed a claim for the loss of his horse, shot from under him in battle:

Camp at San Jacinto
25th April, 1836

Having been called on by Thomas J. Rusk Secretary of War & Col. John A. Wharton to value the horse killed under Major James Collinsworth in battle on the 21st instant, I do therefore value said horse from my own knowledge of his value at three hundred dollars.
James Collinsworth

We approve of the above assessment.
Velasco May 17th 1836 Jno. A. Wharton[2]

James was acting Secretary of State from April 29, 1836 to May 23, 1836. One of his duties during that brief time was to hear the sworn oath of Benjamin C. Franklin as District Judge:[3]

I Benjamin C. Franklin do hereby swear that I will support the Constitution of the Republic of Texas & that I will timely & faithfully demean myself in the office of District Judge for the District of Brazoria during my continuance in office.

May 7th A.D. 1836   *Benj. C. Franklin*
Jas. Collinsworth
Secretary of State

---

[1]. Sam Houston Dixon, *The Men Who Made Texas Free*, (Houston: Texas Historical Society), p 116.

[2]. Republic Claims, *Texas State Library and Archives Commission, Archives &Manuscripts*, Reel 113, Image 73.
http://www.tsl.state.tx.us/arc/repclaims/viewdetails.php?id=22367
Accessed 3/12/2011

[3]. Republic Claims, *Texas State Library and Archives Commission, Archives &Manuscripts*, Reel 33, Image 104.
http://www.tsl.state.tx.us/arc/repclaims/viewdetails.php?id=22367
Accessed 3/12/2011

The Aftermath of San Jacinto[1]

During the battle of San Jacinto and several days prior, President Burnet, Vice-President de Zavala and a few others of the new government had retreated to Galveston. Upon learning the news of the victory at San Jacinto, they left for the Texan camp. President Burnet described his visit: "As soon as the steamer *Yellow Stone* could procure a supply of wood, taking two or three days, I set out in that boat with more provisions and arrived at Buffalo Bayou about the first day of May. Camp had been moved further up the bayou to escape the offensive odors of the battle ground. I found President Santa Anna and his suite occupying the only building in the vicinity. The stern asperities of war were softened down and the more bland and delightful association of peace had resumed its sway where lately bayonets bristled and cannon roared."

President Burnet reported that the worthy Vice-President de Zavala had arrived several days earlier, and that James Collinsworth, the newly inducted Secretary of State, was there also. Secretary of the Treasury Hardeman had also reached the camp ahead of Burnet. Secretary of War Rusk had been in camp with the Army for several weeks, and had been involved, along with General Houston, in negotiations with Santa Anna. Peter Grayson, the Attorney General, was also present. The cabinet met soon after President Burnet's arrival; the great battle and the consequences flowing and to flow from it, were soon introduced as subjects of deliberation.

According to President Burnet, Secretary of War Rusk had already written out in pencil the formula of a treaty with Santa Anna when he arrived, with input from Houston. President Burnet used this treaty as the basis for the one that would be formally drawn up and signed by Santa Anna and himself. Vice-President de Zavala presented and interpreted the treaty to Santa Anna and reported to the Government that the Mexican General was satisfied with it, but desired it to be divided into two separate treaties. He wanted the articles dealing with the recognition and independence of Texas and her boundaries to be included in a second treaty which would not be generally known until he could be reinstated in power and secure the treaty's final ratification.

On May 5, the president and his cabinet, General Houston, Santa Anna and his suite proceeded on the *Yellow Stone* to Galveston Island and then to Velasco on the *Independence* due to lack of facilities on Galveston Island.

---

[1]. Mary Whalley Clark, *David G. Burnet*, (Austin & New York: The Pemberton Press, 1964), pp 107-108; 114-116.

Chapter 7: The Battle of San Jacinto

While at Velasco the Texas government signed the treaty with Santa Anna on May 14, which among other things provided that Santa Anna should be sent to Vera Cruz.

The Signature Page of the "Secret" Treaty of Velasco

The Texas News reported a summary of the treaty signed after the Battle of San Jacinto:

Velasco, May 14, 1836. The ad interim government established here several days ago today signed a treaty with Antonio Lopez de Santa Anna. Known as the treaty of Velasco, the agreement contains ten articles and provides for the following: an immediate end to all hostilities and the retirement of the Mexican Army beyond the Rio Grande; payment by Mexico for all goods and supplies taken by the Mexican army during its retreat; the restoration of all slaves, cattle horses, and other property taken by the Mexican army; the release of all Texan prisoners and of an equal number of Mexican prisoners; the remaining Mexican prisoners to be treated with due humanity; and release of Santa Anna as soon as it is deemed proper. David Burnet, James Collinsworth, Bailey Hardeman, and Peter W. Grayson signed the agreement in behalf of the Texan government. Mirabeau B. Lamar, Secretary of War, refused to sign it, as he favors the immediate execution of Santa Anna and considers the agreement worthless.[1]

The Mob at Velasco[2]

On June 1, in compliance with the terms of the treaty, Santa Anna and his suite went on board the Texas naval vessel *Invincible* at Velasco in preparation for sailing to Vera Cruz.

But before the *Invincible* could get away due to weather, two vessels from New Orleans landed 250 fresh volunteers at Velasco. Among them were Thomas Jefferson Green, J. Pinckney Henderson, and Memucan Hunt – all destined to acquire the title general and to play important roles in Texian history. The new comers had come to Texas to fight, and they thought they had found their chance.

Led by the newly arrived volunteers, the mob that had earlier clamored for Santa Anna surrounded the little shanty that served as the Texian White House. The president came out, looked the leaders of the armed men straight in the eye, and informed them that the treaty with Santa Anna would be fulfilled, and that the faith of Texas preserved. Secretary Grayson told them the same thing in different words. The mob was getting restless. They wanted action, not oratory.

Colonel John A. Wharton, who had been Houston's adjutant general at San Jacinto, pushed his way to the front. A treaty had been made, he told the crowd, and it was a good treaty. But whether good or bad, the treaty was no concern of the army. A soldier's business is to obey the orders of civil authority, not dictate policies. Texas would be no better than Mexico if the army should dictate to the government.

"And you, whom we welcomed hardly an hour ago as comrades in arms! Have you come here to overthrow our government or to help sustain it?" he demanded. "Do you suppose the Texians who have fought and won their right to govern themselves are going to tolerate the dictation of strangers, whether officers or soldiers, just landed on our shores? I for one will assure you here and now that we do not intend to let you become dictators of this country and set our government at defiance!" The answer of the mob was to call again for Santa Anna.

---

[1]. Ralph W. Steen, Editor, The Texas News, (Austin: The Steck Company), p 49.

[2]. Herbert P. Gambrell, *Mirabeau Buonaparte Lamar*, (Dallas: Southwest Press, 1934), pp 106-109.

Secretary Collinsworth rose to speak. A drunken sot yelled: "Put a cap over that man's eyes and string him up!" The crowd took up the cry, and Collinsworth crawled down from the box on which he was about to speak.
Then Secretary Lamar, his eyes flashing with indignation, jumped up to rebuke the mob.

"Major Collinsworth was one of the cabinet who signed the Treaty, and he has a right to be heard in justification of his course," he shouted at the yelling mob. "Furthermore, let me say that if any man here is entitled to an opinion on the disposition of Santa Anna, it is Collinsworth. He helped capture him!" The crowd caught that, and quieted.

"Major Collinsworth and Colonel Wharton fought at San Jacinto! Their counsels and motives are good and pure. You will pardon me, gentlemen, if I think that they are as pure patriots as any newcomer could be supposed to be!" And with his face still flushed with anger, Lamar stepped down.

"Collinsworth! Collinsworth!" yelled the crowd. "Let's hear Major Collinsworth!" But Collinsworth refused now to speak. "Colonel Lamar! Colonel Lamar!" called the crowd.

Lamar remarked to the man beside him, "I have nothing more to say. Mixing in scenes like this doesn't appeal to me."

"Lamar! Lamar!" the crowd kept calling. "Lamar! Read us that letter to the cabinet! Lamar! Lamar! The letter!"

The Secretary of War, still protesting, was hustled to the platform. The crowd became strangely silent. Before them was their man – the member of the Cabinet who wanted to hang Santa Anna.

"You know what my sentiments were when this matter was before the cabinet," he began; and to refresh their memories he read extracts from his letter to President Burnet, while the crowd cheered. When he had finished reading he paused, put his papers back into his pocket, and faced the crowd.

"These were my views as a member of the cabinet; these views I would declare again, under similar circumstances," he said quietly, amidst applause. "But, my friends, the issue is not the same issue that then had to be determined. A Treaty has since been made; our national Faith is pledged in behalf of that Treaty and, I for one, am for carrying all its provisions into full effect!"

The Crowd was stunned. Above the confusion, those who were still listening could hear the Secretary of War vouching for the patriotism and high purpose of President Burnet. "Be calm and use your judgment," Lamar told them. "Mobs must not intimidate the government. We want no French Revolution in Texas!"

As for me, I would rather a thousand Santa Annas should be released; that the battle of San Jacinto should be fought over a hundred times, than to see the military domineering over the government of the country!"

Resignation as acting Secretary of state[1]

Although James had only been in Texas for fifteen months, in a letter to the President and Cabinet, dated Velasco, May 13, 1836, in which he tendered his resignation as acting secretary of state, he indicated that one of the reasons that prompted his resignation was the Government's recently conferring "the highest office in your gift, such as foreign minister, Brigadier General, foreign agencies and many other appointments upon persons who have never been in the country except temporarily upon speculations, injurious to its best interests, to the exclusion of many better qualified who had taken up their permanent residence among you & done the State some service." The references here are probably to the appointment of Childress as commissioner to the United States, of Green as brigadier general, and of Triplett as financial agent.

There is no doubt that James had rendered Texas a distinct service, but further in his letter he indicated that he himself had come to Texas only to help win the revolution and then to return to Tennessee. He wrote:

> *I left the place of my nativity about fifteen months ago with the intention of returning in a short time to settle considerable business which I had on hand both of a publick & private nature. Sickness in the first place & the interest I felt in your struggles for Liberty afterwards, has detained me, up to this period. And without claiming to merit applause, I shall be more than satisfied for the little I have done either in the field or the cabinet should I escape just ground of censure. The result however has been to bring upon me considerable pecuniary loss at home and absolute indigence here, having expended what little of means I brought with me and accumulated some debts without having ever called or received one cent in any way whatever or one acre of land from the government, while many in your country arriving here long since I did & performing no publick services have received large grants of the most valuable lands in your country.*

---

[1]. Louis Wiltz Kemp, *The Signers of the Texas Declaration of Independence*, (Salado Texas: The Anson Jones Press, 1959), pp 82-83.

Chapter 7: The Battle of San Jacinto

Battle of San Jacinto Monument

Chapter 8 - Commissioner to the United States

About a month had passed since the Battle of San Jacinto and two weeks after James' resignation as Secretary of State, President Burnet and the new Secretary of State, William J. Jack, addressed a joint letter to James Collinsworth and Peter W. Grayson[1] appointing them commissioners to the United States. James had very high hopes for success in this role because of his long-term relationship with President Jackson. Their primary goal was to secure the role of the U. S. as mediator in bringing an end to the war between Texas and Mexico on terms recognizing independence. Secondly, they were to indicate to the United States that the annexation of Texas to it would be highly acceptable to the people of Texas.[2]

The Texas News set very high expectations for the two Tennesseans:
Velasco, May 26, 1836. The government today named Peter W. Grayson and James Collinsworth as agents to the United States

---

[1]. Peter Wagener Grayson (1788–1838) was born in Bardstown, Virginia (later Kentucky), in 1788. His family had been prominent in Virginia; his great-uncle William was president of the Continental Congress and a United States senator; he was also related to President James Monroe. Grayson became an attorney, a well-known poet, and also a soldier during the War of 1812. In 1825 he moved to Louisville, from where in 1828 he was elected as a Jacksonian to the state legislature.

During the 1820s Grayson suffered serious mental illness. Temporary recovery came by 1830, when he received a league of land in Stephen F. Austin's Texas colony. By 1832 he had settled and developed a large plantation near Matagorda and had also become a confidant of Austin. In time he had substantial landholdings and owned many slaves. When Austin was imprisoned in Mexico City, Grayson and Spencer H. Jack journeyed there in late 1834 to procure his release.

During the early stages of the Texas Revolution Grayson helped raise volunteers in the United States. On May 4, 1836, president ad interim David Burnet named him attorney general; he signed the Treaties of Velasco on May 14. Two weeks later he and James were named commissioners to the United States to seek recognition and annexation. Texas president Sam Houston named Grayson attorney general in February 1837; he served until leaving for Washington in August as special envoy for annexation. In December 1837 the president made him naval agent to the United States.
[http://www.tshaonline.org/handbook/online/articles/fgr29 Accessed 3/15/2011]

[2]. Walter Prescott Webb, Editor-In-Chief, *Handbook of Texas, Vol 1*, (Austin: Texas State Historical Association, 1952), p 377.

for the purpose of obtaining recognition of Texas independence from the American government. In view of the great friendship for Texas which now exists in the United States, the two agents expect to have little difficulty. Daniel Webster and John C. Calhoun have already spoken publicly in favor of Texas recognition.[1]

On June 6 the *Independence* left Velasco for New Orleans with commissioners Collinsworth and Grayson aboard, reaching that city in seven days. On June 13 its arrival was announced by [Commodore] Hawkins' favorite salute of thirteen guns. They were fully clothed with power to negotiate with the United States government for recognition of the independence of Texas, and left New Orleans the next day for Washington for that purpose.[2]

While James Collinsworth and Peter Grayson were en route to Washington City, the following letter dated June 27, 1836 from John T. Collinsworth to his sister Parmelia Ann Collinsworth Davis gives her an update on their relatives in Texas:

New Orleans
27 June 1836

Dear Sister
I am still at New Orleans. I arrived here on the 11th and am not off to Texas yet. I think, possibly, I shall depart on a vessel to Belasco tomorrow or the day after. I was only fourteen days from Winnebago to this place and this is the sixteenth day that I have been here, the hottest place and the hottest weather I have ever experienced.

I met James here direct from Texas on his way to Washington City. Before he left Texas a truce of a cessation of hostilities was agreed upon between Gen. Santa Anna (now a prisoner in the hands of the Texans) and the Texan Government. But we have lately heard that the Mexican government has not sanctioned the Armistice and is making great preparations for war. The Texans are also making vigorous preparations to repel the attack. People are going there constantly to join the cause and I am in hopes that by the time that Mexico is enabled to send her army against us that we shall not only be able to repulse them but to carry the war into Mexico until they will be glad to agree to fair and honorable terms of peace.

---

[1]. Ralph W. Steen, Editor, <u>The Texas News</u>, (Austin: The Steck Company), p 52.

[2]. Alex Dienst, *The Navy of the Republic of Texas,* George P. Garrison, Editor, The Quarterly of the Texas State Historical Association, Vol. 12, April 1909, p 268.

Chapter 8: Commissioner to the United States

I have every reason to believe that I shall do much better than if I had remained in the U. S. Army and that if I live and have my health I have no doubt but that I shall make a fortune and from what I have learned of Texas it will be one of the most delightful climates on earth to live in as soon as the war is over, which I think will not last long.

Brother James left here last Wednesday for the East. Cousin George Collinsworth is in Texas now and I understand is about to be married. There was no Collinsworth killed in Texas but David C. as I told you in a former letter. I can learn nothing of brother George. However, I inquired of James about him and he told me that he expected he was dead and I am inclined to the same opinion because if he had been living I think we would certainly have heard of him. Though it is painful for us to think of his disappearing in the way he did it cannot be helped and is one of the afflictions which is frequently visited on the human family and it may all be for the best, at any rate, it is our duty to submit to such dispensations with fortitude and resignation.

Remember me to Sister Susan and Elizabeth and to all our friends and relatives and ever my love to Marthy Thull. Tell Mr. Davis I would like to have a line or two from him now and then. Direct your letters to me at Belasco, Texas via New Orleans and the postage must be paid or they will not be sent to Texas.

Until you hear from me again be assured that I am most sincerely your affectionate brother.
J. T. Collinsworth[1]

The trip from Velasco to New Orleans to Washington City was long and difficult, taking a total of 31 days. A letter from the Commissioners to President Burnet explains why they were late arriving and gave their alternate plans to make their mission as successful as possible:

To His Ex[cellency] D.G. Burnet[2]
Pres[ident] At H[ouston].
Washington 15th July 1836

Sir
We arrived here on the 7th inst, after having been detained, some days on consequence, of low water, & getting aground in the Ohio River. [W]e

---

[1]. Transcription of a letter received from Caroline Davis Tate, a descendant of James' sister Parmelia.
[2]. James Collinsworth and Peter Grayson to David G. Burnet, July 15, 1836. Executive Records Books, Texas Secretary of State, Archives and Information Services Division, Texas State Library and Archives Commission.

omitted no ordinary exertions, to reach this place, before the adjournment of Congress, but by unavoidable delays were disappointed.

On arriving here, we were informed that the President of the U. States, was on the point of setting out for the Hermitage, and that time would not admit of a formal interview. Under these circumstances (Congress having adjourned and most of the members left) one of us having had a long personal acquaintance with the President, deemed it not improper, on the evening of our arrival to make a personal call, during which we were fairly led to infer from a conversation with him, that he had sent a Secret Agent on the part of the Government of the United States to Texas, with letters to the President of the Republic to prosecute various inquiries, on to our situation internal, civil & political, and that nothing conclusive could be done until that commissioner was heard from.

We have had two interviews with Mr. Forsyth[1], since the departure of the President, and find him but little disposed to be communicative, in anything, but he has conversed with us in regard to the objects of our mission, and has stated that he knew the annexation of Texas, to the U. States, was a favourite measure of Genl. Jackson[']s, whenever it could be done with propriety. He informs us, that he has forwarded to General Jackson, at the Hermitage, the Terms, so far as disclosed by us, forwarded on our instructions, upon which an incorporation of Texas, with the United States, would be acceptable to the former[,] and that he could do nothing upon the Subject until the opinions & actions of the President are had thereon. Under these circumstances, it will be useless to remain during the Summer.

One of us, P.W Grayson, will therefore return in a short time to Louisville [KY] and the other to Nashville Tennessee, where they will both hold themselves ready, to receive any instructions, or obey any commands of their Government.

Should it be desired that we should longer represent our Government here, it will be necessary to make out new commissions & forward them to the last named places, as those we have, have been deemed inadmissible in consequence of having no seal.

It will be seen by reference to our constitution, that in the absence of a Seal of State, the President is allowed to use his private seal. There is a further omission, in the address to the Secretary of State, & the President, even of the country it is from. He [Forsyth] knows the difficulty of recollecting all these things without forms. [W]e merely name them to prevent the possibility of their being overlooked.

Very Respectfully yr Servts
J. Collinsworth
P.W. Grayson

---

[1]. U.S. Secretary of State John Forsyth.

Chapter 8: Commissioner to the United States

Forsyth suggested to them that they write him a private letter setting forth the essential terms of their instructions. This they did, stating the terms on which the annexation of Texas to the United States would be highly acceptable to the people of Texas.[1]

While they were in the east, Collinsworth and Grayson continued on to other cities, promoting Texas and seeking funding for the fledgling republic. In a letter from Columbia Texas, dated December 12, 1836, Ira Randolph Lewis, states, "*In New York I had the pleasure of meeting one of the last commissioners sent out by President Burnet, viz., our distinguished and worthy fellow-citizen, James Collinsworth, just as I was on the eve of leaving that city*".[2]

A letter from Peter Grayson to Secretary of State Wm. H. Jack reports further details of their travels and, although omitted here, gave descriptions of ships being built in Baltimore for the Mexican government, along with suggestions on how to intercept the ships when completed:

Washington [City,] July 30, 1836

Dr Sir,

> *Leaving this place with Majr. Collinsworth a few days ago on a short trip to Philadelphia, and passing through Baltimore, we took pains to obtain all the information possible in regard to two brigs of War, we understood the Mexican Government, by their Agent, were having built there, for immediate service in the gulf.*
>
> *I doubt not that through the late Commissioners, our Government has already received some account of these Vessels [sic]; Genl. Austin particularly when in Balto. having obtained information of them, from a person residing there, who was well acquainted with everything, in regard to them.*
>
> *As he, however could only speak of their state of forwardness, at the time he left, which is now something upwards of two months ago, I consider it important (Majr. Collinsworth being at present absent at N York) without delay to communicate what I know of their present condition, with my conjecture as to the time in which they will probably be completed. Having been, no later than yesterday, on board of one of them and but a few days before, seen the other, I am able of course to give certain information with respect to them...*
>
> *... What I have written I submit of course with proper deference to the judgment of my Government. Little Versed as I am in such subjects I*

---

[1]. Eugene C. Barker, *President Jackson and the Texas Revolution in The American Historical Review*, Vol 12 No. 4, (July, 1907) pp 805-806.
[2]. John Henry Brown, *Indian Wars and Pioneers of Texas*, (Austin TX: L. E. Daniell, Publisher, 1880), p 175.

would only be considered as offering suggestions which I know run some risk of being of no value. The mere chance however of their being something of a different character will I think serve as my excuse for making them.

After all it may be that some far better plan has been already thought of for the object in view. Nevertheless if I shall ascertain or think of anything further on the subject which I shall think important to be known I will not fail to communicate it immediately. That something effectual may be done in the matter, I anxiously hope; for I give it as my opinion, that these Vessels would be able to clear the gulph [sic] of the whole of our Navy.

I enclose a Duplicate of the Communication made by Majr. Collinsworth and myself to the Government, on the 15th inst. This I do to meet the contingency of the Original having miscarried.

Nearly all the Heads of Departments are at present absent from the city.

As soon as Majr. Collinsworth arrives here, which will be in a day or two, we will depart for our respective temporary destinations Louisville and Nashville,

I have the honor to be
Very respectfully
Yr Obt Servt
    P W. Grayson
[To]
Honble Wm H. Jack
Secretary of State etc etc [1]

While James was traveling in the east as commissioner, his brother, Lt. John T. Collinsworth, resigned from the U.S. Army, 5th Infantry on July 31, 1836, to join the Texian Army.[2]

James left Washington on August 4 and followed Jackson to the Hermitage, calling several times, unsuccessfully, on President Jackson.[3]

---

[1]. George P. Garrison, Editor, *Annual report of the American Historical Association for the Year 1907, Volume 2, Part I* (Washington: Government Printing Office, 1908), pp 114-116.

[2]. B. Homans, *The Army and Navy Chronicle,* Vol. 4, B. Homans, Washington, 1837, p 127.

[3]. Herbert P. Gambrell, *Anson Jones, The Last President of Texas*, University of Texas Press, Second Edition, Austin, p 121.

Chapter 8: Commissioner to the United States

While he was still in Nashville James received the following letter[1] from President Burnet giving him details of the recent election in Texas:

Executive Department
Velasco 12 Sept. 1836

To Hon
James Collinsworth

Dear Sir
I had the pleasure to receive your letter of 15 July apprising us of your arrival in Washington, etc etc. I trust you have availed yourself of every opportunity to make a favorable impression on the mind of the venerable President of the U.S. Your long personal acquaintance with him gives you many facilities for this purpose.

Our elections are over and there is no doubt that Genl. Houston is the President elect—Lamar, vice P., Wm H. Wharton is probably [chosen] for the Senate. John A. W[harton] and Dr. Archer lower house. The meeting of Congress is so near at hand that I do not think advisable to anticipate that time in the appointment of an Agent for Washington. One at least will doubtless be appointed soon after its assemblage in haste.

your Obt. Sev't
Signed
David G. Burnet

Only five months after the victory over Santa Anna, the hero of San Jacinto had won election to the presidency by a huge margin over Stephen F. Austin and Henry Smith. Bankrupt and lawless, Texas was teetering on the edge of disintegration. Provisional president Burnet resigned so that Houston could take office early on October 22, 1836.

At his inauguration in Columbia, Houston dramatically flourished, then gave up the sword he had used at the Battle of San Jacinto. It was a symbolic gesture by which Houston hoped to signal to the people that it was time to turn away from war and to the business of building a new Texas. The same day that Houston was inaugurated James left Nashville for Texas.

In his letter making a claim to the Republic of Texas for service during the revolution, Charles De Morse reports the officials he observed en route from New Orleans to Velasco:[2]

---

[1]. George P. Garrison, *Diplomatic Correspondence of the Republic of Texas, Part I*: Annual Report of the American Historical Association for the year 1907, Vol. II, (Washington, Government Printing Office, 1908), p 123.

[2]. Republic Claims, *Texas State Library and Archives Commission, Archives &Manuscripts,* Reel 113, Image 74.
http://www.tsl.state.tx.us/arc/repclaims/viewdetails.php?id=22367
Accessed 3/12/2011

> *The Independence was ordered to New Orleans for supplies and increase of men, sufficient for her armament and while there in July [1836], your applicant saw in the public journals, the calls of General Rusk for volunteers to repel the invasion by Filisola. Your applicant determined to seek field service, and within an hour after anchoring in the harbor of Velasco resigned his commission in the marines and went on shore to make his way to the army. There he found a party preparing for the trip and moved with them as soon as they were prepared.*
>
> *On this return trip from New Orleans, the Independence brought home William H. Wharton and Branch T. Archer who with Stephen F. Austin had been returning as Commissioners for Texas, appointed to enlist the co-operation of the government of the United States in assisting our struggle for Independence. On board also, were Peter W. Grayson, subsequently a candidate for President of Texas, and James Collinsworth, afterwards Chief Justice of the Supreme Court, and his brother, afterwards Inspector General of the Army.*

From Velasco James returned to Brazoria and his law practice accompanied by his brother, John. After the battle of San Jacinto Anson Jones had returned to his medical practice in Brazoria only to find that, according to Jones, "two lawyers had 'squatted' in one room of my office and I was unable to get them out for several weeks; when I succeeded it produced a "challenge" from my friend the Chief Justice J. Collinsworth, which I accepted, to fight with pistols at ten steps. It was, however, settled, his object having been to "bluff," which, when he found out it would not succeed, he got his friend T. F. McKinney to get him out of the scrape."[1]

At this time poorly trained lawyers may have made up the largest portion of the legal profession of the Republic, but there were some very talented individual attorneys with genuine claims to distinction in the profession. San Augustine and Brazoria Counties, for example, boasted Bars that would have been noteworthy anywhere in the Southern States.[2]

The Republic of Texas had no law library worthy of the name; but some individual practitioners possessed private libraries of substantial size. Those of Thomas J. Rusk, James Collinsworth and William Fairfax Gray were especially noteworthy.[3]

---

[1]. Herbert Pickens Gambrell, *Anson Jones, The Last President of Texas*, University of Texas Press, Austin, *Second Edition, 1964, pp 86-87.*

[2]. Joe E. Ericson, *Judges of the Republic of Texas*, (Dallas: Taylor, 1980), p 13.

[3]. Joe E. Ericson, *Judges of the Republic of Texas*, (Dallas: Taylor, 1980), p 13.

Chapter 8: Commissioner to the United States

James had been in Brazoria less than a month when he made his final report in a letter[1] to now President Houston regarding his trip as Commissioner to the United States:

Brazoria
Nov. 13th, 1836

To the President of the Republic of Texas,

Sir, the undersigned, in conjunction with P. W. Grayson Esqr. was appointed on the second day of June last, commissioners on the part of this government to the court of Washington. The duties with which they were charged will appear by a record of their credentials and instructions on file in the office of the Secretary of State.

They accordingly repaired with as little delay as possible to Washington City. When they arrived there they found congress adjourned and the President of the United States on the point of setting out for the Hermitage. The undersigned impressed with the importance of an interview with him previous to his departure from the seat of government, called on him immediately. He briefly informed me that nothing could be done until he heard from an agent despatched [sic] from the government of the U. States to the government of Texas to inquire into the civil and political condition of the latter country. But referred us to Mr. Forsyth Secretary of State for all further communication on the subject. We saw Mr. Forsyth and presented our credentials, they were formally objected to for the omission of the seal of the State being affixed to them. We immediately wrote to the President of this Republick informing him of the fact and requesting him either to supply the omission or grant us leave to return. Informing him also that the undersigned would repair [one] to Nashville and the other to Louisville and await orders.

A short time afterwards it was deemed more expedient that one should remain at Washington as something might arrive or occur that would render even an unauthorized agent of Texas useful at that place. Upon consultation between Mr. Grayson and myself it was determined that he should remain at Washington and that I would repair to Nashville where I would be more likely to have an opportunity of discussing the objects of my mission with the President himself, at the Hermitage to advantage than even at Washington. I accordingly repaired to the former place and Saw him frequently while there. He informed me in substance that nothing could be done until the Congress of Texas met and organized a more formal and regular government, than that then in existence. Deeming myself without power to act and anxiously awaiting

---

[1]. George P. Garrison, Editor, *Annual report of the American Historical Association for the Year 1907, Volume 2, Part I* (Washington: Government Printing Office, 1908), pp125-126.

the orders of my government, I determined to remain at Nashville until I could hear from the President of this Republick.

On the 21st of Oct last I rec'd the enclosed letter marked A. which I considered as finally ending any pretence of authority on my part to act as an agent of this government," and I accordingly set out for this place the next day.

It might be further necessary to state that previous to the arrival of the letter last referred to: I had addressed a letter to the President of the U. States a copy of which if desired I will furnish, briefly setting forth the objects, powers and policy of the subjects with which I was charged.

Without pretending to have received any official information upon the subject, which of course I could not do for the reason above stated, I think [I] may safely hazard the opinion that the present ex[ec]utive of the United States is in favor of all the measures contained in our instructions. Should the present government believe in the same policy, I cannot too forcibly impress upon them the necessity of despatching [sic] someone forthwith vested with plenary powers to the court of Washington, as in my opinion much may be endangered by delay to bring these matters before the approaching session of the Congress of the United States at an early period of its session.

With this brief view of the subject I remain your ob't ser't.

Jas. Collinsworth.

Two days later Houston wrote this note to the Senate with James' report firmly sewed to Houston's message.

Executive Department, Columbia, 15th Novr, 1836[1]

To the Honorable Senate:

I have the honor to transmit to you the report of the Hon. James Collinsworth, one of the late Commissioners from this Government to the City of Washington.

It contains a succint [sic] account of his reception and doings in our behalf, and of the prospects which may await a duly empowered minister fully accredited. His opinion in regard to the propriety of dispatching such an envoy to the United States, clothed with complete authority to negotiate with that Nation upon the interesting subject of our nationality and relations, is well worthy [of] your attention— And I cannot forebear

---

[1]. Messages of the Presidents," *Congressional Papers*, Texas State Library. Firmly sewed to Houston's message to the Senate was Collinsworth's report. It is printed in Garrison (ed.), Texas Diplomatic Correspondence, I, 125-126.

Chapter 8: Commissioner to the United States

my reiterated assurance that all the ends of our social happiness are to be promoted by that measure.

It is due to the character of those gentlemen to state that as commissioners, they have reflected credit upon their fellow citizens, and have acquitted themselves faithfully so far as the total want of necessary powers would admit.

Sam Houston [Rubric]

More than a year would pass after James' return to Texas from Washington and Nashville before he was paid for his service as commissioner to the United States:

Joint Resolution[1]
For the Relief of James Collinsworth.

Resolved; by the senate and house of representatives of the republic of Texas, in congress assembled, that the treasurer be, and is hereby authorized to pay James Collinsworth three thousand dollars, or so much as may remain due him, of that amount, being for his services as commissioner to the United States; that being the salary established by a law of the consultation passed at San Felipe on the 8th December A. D. 1835.

Joseph Rowe, Speaker of the House of Representatives.
S. H. Everitt, President pro tem of the Senate.

Approved Dec. 18, 1837.
Sam. Houston.

Lt. John T. Collinsworth became acting Inspector General of the army from 31 October, 1836 to 22 December, 1836 at which time he would be nominated by President Houston to Inspector General.[2] On the same day that James had made his report to President Houston of his activities as commissioner, John T. Collinsworth wrote a letter to their sister, Parmelia Ann Collinsworth Davis.

Brazerio, Texas
13 November 1836

Dear Sister

---

[1]. Telegraph and Texas Register, (Houston, TX), February 24, 1838.
[2]. E. W. Winkler (ed.), *Secret Journals of the Senate, Republic of Texas, 1836-1845*, 40-41.

Your letter written last summer during Mr. Davis' absence was received and I should have answered it sooner but ill health and the want of the means of writing prevented me while in camp. I was sick during the month of August and part of September but since I have been in good health with the exception of a slight chill and fever on two or three occasions which only lasted two or three days.

I suppose you have heard that I arrived in Texas at Velasco early in July the 7, 8, or 9th of the month, I do not recollect which, at present. During the month of July I was in perfect health. During that part of the summer I remained in this part of Texas and about the first of August I went to the Army stationed about 120 miles west of this place. I was ordered to Columbia, now the seat of government of this republic, and about 12 miles from this place. About three or four weeks since I am now Major of Infantry and Assistant Adjutant General with the rank of major in the staff. The congress of Texas is not in session and I understand a bill has proposed the reorganization of the army and I have been assured that I should receive the commission of Colonel. There is no immediate prospect of the Mexicans attacking us.

James has arrived in Texas and is now in this place. I never saw him in better health in my life. I am glad to hear that you are all well. I am very well pleased with the country. It is as good in every respect as I expected and in some, better. I presume that I shall enjoy my health as well here as in the states after I become acclimated. And I am convinced that I can do better here than in any part of the States. If I live and have my health I feel certain of making a fortune here, and I shall, I think, certainly gain as much fame as I should in my mother country and besides this country may and, I think it probably will, be one of the United States before very long and then the state of Texas will be considered the choice state of all the southern states.

There is a law before congress extending the bounty lands to those who have come to Texas since the first of July and making it equal to those who came before and if this bill should pass into law it will be something into my pocket.

I am very much grieved to say that not one half of the letters written to and from Texas ever reach their place of destination because there are some unprincipled villains who make it their business to open all letters in which they suppose they can find any money and sometimes no doubt to gratify their idle curiosity.

As soon as the wars are over I am in hopes of having an opportunity of visiting you all but if I do before, it will be owing to some consequence unforeseen at present.

Remember me to all our friends and relatives. Tell them I never forget the land of my birth nor my old friends. You will probably see by the papers that brother James was appointed one of the Cabinet but on his arrival he declined accepting the appointment.

Chapter 8: Commissioner to the United States

I wish you and all our friends would write whenever you can. Direct your letters to Brazerio, Texas in the care of Toby and Brother, New Orleans. I grant it is very discouraging to write and have to pay the postage and then for your letters to run about equal chances not to be received but I regret to say they are the terms at present and I assure you that when I receive a letter written under so many unfavorable circumstances I shall value it the more highly.

That Heaven may protect you and shower its blessing upon you and yours is the earnest prayer and wish of your friend and brother.

J. T. Collinsworth[1]

---

[1]. Transcription of a letter received from Caroline Davis Tate, a descendant of James' sister Parmelia.

Chapter 9 – Wealth and Fame at Last

Election to the Senate of the Republic of Texas

The first session of the first congress of the Republic of Texas convened in October, 1836 at Columbia, now West Columbia.

On October 26, 1836, President Houston appointed James Collinsworth Attorney General of the Republic, but he declined to accept the office owing to pressing personal business. However, when William H. Wharton resigned as a member of the First Senate to accept an appointment as Minister to the United States, James was elected from the Brazoria District to the First Congress to fill the vacancy expiring September 3, 1838.[1]

On Wednesday, November 30, 1836, Mr. Everett from the committee on privileges and elections reported that Jas. Collinsworth, Esq. was duly elected from the district of Brazoria a senator to fill the vacancy occasioned by the resignation of the Hon. Wm. H. Wharton. Mr. Irion moved a committee be appointed to wait on the Hon. James Collinsworth, and inform him of his election, and invite him to a seat in the senate; which motion was adopted, and the chair announced Messrs. Irion, Wilson, and Everett said committee.[2] James was seated on November 30, 1836.[3]

Petition to Charter the Texas Railroad, Navigation and Banking Company

James' timely election to the senate brought an opportunity to launch a major business venture in the fledgling republic. Citing immediate need for land and water transportation along with local financing and investments, the founders prepared the petitions they would present to the Senate and the House. An article in The Southwestern Historical Quarterly records the petition for charter, except as noted:[4]

---

[1]. Telegraph and Texas Register, (Columbia, TX), Vol. 1, No. 44, Ed. 1, Tuesday, December 6, 1836.

[2]. Telegraph and Texas Register, (Columbia, TX), Vol. 1, No. 44, Ed. 1, Tuesday, December 6, 1836

[3]. Patsy McDonald Spaw, *The Texas Senate: Republic to Civil War, 1836-1861*, Texas A&M University Press, 1991, (*Senate Journal*, First Congress, First Session, p. 66).

[4]. Andrew Forest Muir, *The Southwestern Historical Quarterly, Vol. XLVII, APRIL, 1944, No. 4.*

On Friday, December 9, 1836, Congressman Thomas J. Green[1] presented to the First Congress of the Republic of Texas a petition of Congressman Archer and Senator Collinsworth to charter the Texas Railroad, Navigation and Banking Company. The petition artfully described the company's lofty goals and expected results:

The undersigned Citizens of this Republic, feeling as they should, the liveliest interest in the welfare and prosperity of their country, by the suggestions of other patriotic and enterprising gentlemen, most respectfully pray that your honorable body will grant them a charter privilege for connecting the waters of the Rio Grande, by internal navigation and railroads, with the waters of the Sabine.

A few remarks upon the importance of this work, its commercial, as well as national advantages may not be inapplicable at present.

A slight glance at the geographical position of this route will show its entire practicability. Its commercial advantages extending from one extreme of the Republic, to the other, in times of peace, will be incalculable, in times of war, indispensible. Affording at all times a safe internal communication from one extreme eastern border to the heart of the great Valley of the Rio Grande--making the extremes, neighbours, and uniting the whole together as one great family. In time of war, when a superior marine enemy shall close our ports and blockade our whole coast, we will have a great high road among ourselves, and a free and undisturbed communication to our great eastern neighbour.

Your petitioners further believe that with the advantages of such a work, a few steam Frigates adapted to our bays, would render us

---

[1]. Thomas Jefferson Green, soldier, was born in Warren county, N.C., Feb. 14, 1802; son of Solomon and Fanny (Hawkins) Green. He attended Chapel Hill College and the U.S. military Academy. In 1822 he was elected to the general assembly of North Carolina and shortly after was married to Sarah A., daughter of the Hon. Jesse Wharton of Nashville, Tenn. He then removed to a plantation in Florida, where he remained till the death of his wife in 1832, having in the meantime represented his county in the Florida legislature. In 1836 he went to Texas, where he was commissioned brigadier-general and sent back to the United States to raise a brigade, which he did at the expense of his entire fortune. Returning with his brigade, he arrived at Velasco after the battle of San Jacinto and on the day that Santa Anna was released and placed on a war vessel to be carried to Vera Cruz, General Green, believing the release of Santa Anna to be a mistake, protested, and trader the authority of President Burnet, reimpressioned the Mexican. This action was sustained by the government and Santa Anna was consigned to the care of General Green, who treated him as a guest. [*The Twentieth Century Biographical Dictionary of Notable Americans: Volume IV*, page 396.]

Chapter 9: Wealth and Fame at Last

invulnerable from any invasion by Sea. If it should please your honorable body to grant such charter with banking privileges, your petitioners are assured of its accomplishment, and the introduction of a large foreign capital, the advantage of which would be necessary to its completion:--& will be incalculable to the present narrow monied means of the Country.

Your petitioners propose as a bonus to the Government, that so soon as the Bank shall go into operation, to pay $25,000. Say Twenty five thousand Dollars, and also Two and one half Per Cent yearly, upon the net profits arising from the tolls and fees of said work, so long as its charter shall continue.

They also propose that the Government shall transport forever free of expense, all soldiers, provisions, ammunitions, and munitions of war, and also all vessels and transports of War.[1]

On December 9 the petition was referred to the Committee on the State of the Republic. The next day Branch T. Archer, Stephen F. Austin, James Collinsworth, James P. Henderson, and Thomas F. McKinney formed a partnership:

We . . . have and by these presents agree in joint partnership and interest and bind ourselves together as co-equal partners to be equally interested in a plan and project of a Banking and internal improvement scheme, to be called the "Texas Railroad Navigation and Banking Company" which charter privilege we ask of the Congress of the Republic of Texas, in the names of Branch T. Archer and James Collinsworth, and which charter if passed into a law, we obligate ourselves each to the other, to take in such other partners as may be agreed upon, in manner and form hereafter to be prescribed, but in all respects to have the same rights and privileges as ourselves in proportion to the number of Shares by each respectively held.[2]

A brief biography of each of James' partners follows:

Branch Tanner Archer[3] (1790–1856) was born in Fauquier County, Virginia. His father, Peter Archer, was a Revolutionary War officer. Branch Archer attended William and Mary College at Williamsburg in 1804, and in 1808 he received his M.D. degree from the medical school at the University of

---

[1]. Petition of B. T. Archer and Jas. Collinsworth, undated. Memorials and Petitions (MSS. in Archives, Texas State Library, Austin). The petition was apparently written shortly before its presentation to Congress.
[2]. Eugene C. Barker (ed.), *The Austin Papers* (Austin, 1926), III, p 472.
[3]. http://www.tshaonline.org/handbook/online/articles/far02 Accessed 3/15/2011

Pennsylvania. After returning to Virginia he practiced medicine, served one or two terms in the Virginia legislature.

Archer arrived in Texas in 1831 and quickly joined a group in Brazoria agitating for independence from Mexico. He represented Brazoria at the Convention of 1833 and participated in the battle of Gonzales in October 1835. In November 1835 he traveled to San Felipe as representative of Brazoria and there was elected chairman of the Consultation.

The Consultation then selected Archer to join Stephen F. Austin and William H. Wharton as commissioners to the United States to lobby for financial assistance, collect supplies, and recruit men for the Texas cause. During their trip Texas declared its independence, on March 2, 1836. The three commissioners were unable to persuade Congress to support their cause and returned home.

After returning to Texas Archer worked for the election of Stephen F. Austin as president of the young republic. He also served in the First Congress of Texas and as speaker of the House during its second session.

Stephen Fuller Austin[1] (1793-1836) known as "The Father of Texas," He established the first Anglo-American colony in the Tejas province of Mexico and saw it grow into an independent republic.

Austin was born in southwestern Virginia, but his family moved to Missouri when he was five years old. After four years of schooling at Yale College, he returned to Missouri, where he had a mixed career as a storekeeper, manager of the family lead mining business, and director of a failed bank. He served as a militia officer and was a member of the Missouri territorial legislature from 1814 to 1820. In 1820, Arkansas' governor appointed him as a circuit judge.

It was Austin's father, Moses Austin, who took the first steps toward establishing an American colony in Mexican Tejas. In 1820, he traveled to San Antonio to petition for a land grant, and in 1821 received approval to settle 300 American families on 200,000 acres. But Moses Austin died before completing his plans and responsibility for establishing the colony fell to Stephen.

Austin selected a site on the lower Colorado and Brazos rivers, and settled his colonists there in January 1822. Almost at once he faced opposition from the newly independent Mexican government, which refused to recognize his father's land grant since it had been made under Spanish charter. Austin traveled to Mexico City to correct this situation, and using skillful diplomacy secured a new law confirming his right to colonize the land and designating him as the new colony's *empresario* or administrative authority.

Austin had mixed success with the Mexican government. President Antonio López de Santa Anna agreed to repeal the 1830 law against further

---

[1] http://www.pbs.org/weta/thewest/people/a_c/austin.htm

Chapter 9: Wealth and Fame at Last

American immigration, but he refused to grant the request for statehood. He also had Austin imprisoned for a time on suspicion of inciting an insurrection.

Even after his release in July 1835, Austin still thought an alliance with Mexican liberals was the best option for Americans in Texas, but the outbreak of the Texas Revolution at Gonzales on October 1, 1835 left him little choice but to support the drive for independence. He took command of the attack on Mexican troops led by Juan Sequin at San Antonio, and then in late 1835 began to act as commissioner to the United States, traveling to Washington to seek military support and the eventual annexation of Texas by the United States. He also sought to rally public support for Texas in speeches delivered along his route.

Austin's efforts in Washington proved unsuccessful, however, and he returned to Texas in June 1836, shortly after the Texas War for Independence had been won at San Jacinto. In the fall, he was defeated in a bid for the presidency by Sam Houston, but he served as secretary of state until his death on December 27, 1836.

James Pinckney Henderson[1] (1808–1858), was born in Lincolnton, North Carolina He attended Lincoln Academy and the University of North Carolina, studied law, and was admitted to the bar in 1829. After serving as aide-de-camp and major in the North Carolina militia in 1830, he was elected colonel of a regiment. He moved to Canton, Mississippi, in 1835, became interested in news of the Texas Revolution, and began enlistments for the Texas service.

He arrived at Velasco, Texas, on June 3, 1836, and was commissioned by David G. Burnet as brigadier general and sent to the United States to recruit for the Texas army. Henderson organized a company in North Carolina and sent it to Texas, reputedly at his own expense. Upon his return to Texas in November 1836, he was appointed attorney general of the republic under Sam Houston and in December 1836 succeeded Stephen F. Austin as Secretary of State.

Early in 1837 Henderson was appointed Texas minister to England and France and was commissioned particularly to secure recognition and treaties of amity and commerce. Largely through his efforts both England and France entered into trade agreements with the republic and ultimately recognized Texas independence. He would become the first governor of the state of Texas.

Thomas Freeman McKinney[2] (1801–1873) was born in Lincoln County, Kentucky and received a common-school education in Christian County,

---

[1]. http://www.tshaonline.org/handbook/online/articles/fhe14 Accessed 3/15/2011

[2]. http://www.tshaonline.org/handbook/online/articles/fmc75 Accessed 3/15/2011

Kentucky, where the family lived from 1811 to 1818. McKinney went to Santa Fe in 1823 and then Chihuahua, Durango, Saltillo, and Bexar. In 1824 he received a league on the Brazos River from Stephen F. Austin, but a trip to Ayish Bayou, where his uncle Stephen Prather had a trading post, convinced him that the Nacogdoches area was best for trade.

In 1830 he moved to San Felipe and continued trading to the south. In 1834 he became senior partner with Samuel May Williams in McKinney and Williams, a firm located on the Brazos; Williams supplied the bookkeeping and commercial contacts in the United States, while McKinney collected and shipped the cotton. The firm developed Quintana at the mouth of the river in 1835 and used its credit to help finance the Texas Revolution to the amount of $99,000, which was never repaid in full.

McKinney obtained a privateering license from the Provisional Government and used the firm's credit to buy the *William Robbins*, renamed *Liberty*, for the rebel government. Though he refused commissions as commissary general and loan agent, he continued to forward men and supplies to the Texas army.

He and Williams joined Menard in 1833 in a scheme to claim Galveston Island, and in 1836 they combined with others to secure a charter for the Galveston City Company. The firm had a wharf and warehouse on the island in October 1837, when Racer's Hurricane struck and severely damaged their property.

On December 13, J. W. Bunton, chairman of the Committee on the State of the Republic, reported on the petition:

The Select Committee to whom was referred an act to incorporate The Texas Rail Road, Navigation and Banking Company, have carefully considered the same, and recommend its passage, with the following amendment: that said bonus of twenty five thousand dollars shall be paid within eighteen months from the incorporation of said company; and in the event of its not being paid within said time said charter shall be forfeited and considered null & void.[1]

Congress concurred in the report and approved the charter, which President Houston signed on December 16, 1836.

Provisions of the Charter

This charter provided that the company should have a capital of five million dollars, banking privileges, and the right to connect by canals and railroads the waters of the Rio Grande with those of the Sabine. The capital stock should be divided into fifty thousand shares of one hundred dollars each. The bank should not go into operation until it had a specie capital of

---

[1]. The amendment was attached to the petition of Archer and Collinsworth.

one million dollars, should not charge a greater discount than ten per cent, and should not issue notes of less than five dollars.

At the beginning of operations of the bank, the company should pay into the treasury of the Republic twenty-five thousand dollars in gold or silver and thereafter two and one-half per cent upon the annual net profits of the canals and railroads and one per cent of the bank dividends. During times of war the company should transport military matériel and personnel without tariff.

The charter was to be in force for forty-nine years, at the end of which time the company should have the privilege of renewing it for a like period, upon paying five hundred thousand dollars in gold or silver to the government, and thereafter five per cent upon the annual net profits. At any time the company might increase the capital stock to ten million dollars.

The charter granted the right of eminent domain and provided that the company might occupy a mile-wide strip through public lands. The bank should be located at any place the company might think proper, and it might establish two branches whenever it wished and more than two upon congressional approval. Every year the president of the Republic should appoint a commissioner to examine the company and to report upon the bonus due the government, and the first bonus should be paid within eighteen months from the passage of the act, or the charter would be forfeited.[1]

On December 20, 1836, the company granted to Stephen F. Austin fifty [actually thirty]-one hundred shares of stock and certified that, in case the capital should be enlarged to ten million dollars, he should be entitled to 3125 additional shares.[2]

Thomas J. Green's Glowing Interpretation of the Charter and His Ideas for the Company as Requested by President Archer.[3]

Columbia, Dec. 26, 1836

To the Hon. B. T. Archer,
President, Texas Rail Road, Navigation and Banking Company.

. . . I have examined your charter with much attention, and find it as liberal in all its provisions, as the company ought to desire, and more so than any other in my recollection.

The privilege of discounting thirty millions of paper, at ten per centum per annum, upon its ten millions capital stock—its unrestricted

---

[1]. H. P. N. Gammel (ed.), *The Laws of Texas, 1822-1897* (Austin, 1898), I, 1188-92.
[2]. Barker (ed.), *The Austin Papers,* III, 477-78.
[3]. Telegraph and Texas Register, (Houston, TX), Vol. 2, No. 36, Ed 1, Saturday, September 16, 1837.

privilege to deal in bills of exchange—its unresisted authority over the establishment of tolls, fees and charges of the works—the privilege of taking, at the minimum government price, all the land within half a mile of such works—its full and ample power and authority to buy and sell all species of property—the advantages of investment at the present low prices of real property—the right that foreign stockholders have to hold real estate in Texas, not otherwise allowed them, together with ninety-eight years duration of charter, are privileges almost incalculable, and are invaluable to the company. On the other hand, the Government will be immensely benefited, not only by the liberal bonus paid for the charter, but by the introduction of large foreign capital, necessary to the present wants of the country; and more than all, by the accomplishment of a magnificent improvement, the completion of which, as proposed, will far exceed any other in the history of nations. . .

But in event of your securing the town site upon the Copano Bay, and the land up the valley of the San Antonio river, one hundred and twenty miles to the city of [San Antonio de] Bexar, and the real property in and near that city, it will not be necessary for you to do more than to survey the road, before millions of property may be sold upon it; for no portion of the earth presents more inducements;--the incomparable richness of the soil and salubrity of the climate of the valley of the San Antonio, is proverbial. It is estimated that from thirty to fifty thousand dollars will turn the Rio Grande into the bay of Brassos Santiago, by a canal of about three miles, upon which bay the great city of that great valley must be built, with a back country to support it six times as large as Pennsylvania. Just above this point, upon the Rio Grande, the stupid, indolent, barbarian people, who inhabit it, have within a few years built the rich city of Matamoros, with only the advantage of five feet water to it. What a city then might not an American people build upon the bay below, where there can be eleven feet brought in?—There are many other sites where towns and cities must be built soon, all within the reach of your charter, which a small improvement would render most valuable.

To confine myself more particularly to the plan, as proposed, let me call your attention to the fact, that less than thirty miles of canal will unite the Sabine lake with the waters of the Rio Grande, with not an elevation in the profile of the whole route of twenty feet, and through a clay of such peculiar tenacity, that the sides of the bayous wherever I have examined them are generally perpendicular. This is alone a sufficient argument upon the practicability of navigating the canals by steam.—This route, which is to form the principle trunk of your whole plan, covers the whole seacoast of the Republic, from east to west, a distance of 400 miles. To make it continuous, it will require three principal cuts—one from East river into a bayou of Sabine lake, of less than a mile; one from West bay to Matagorda, of about 22

Chapter 9: Wealth and Fame at Last

miles; and one from near Point Isabel, upon the bay of Brassos Santiago, to the Rio Grande, of about three miles. . . . The numerous rivers which wind in every direction over the whole face of the country . . . all emptying their rich products into your great parallel reservoir to the sea; many of them, with a small improvement at their mouths, capable of good and constant stream navigation, and almost all a portion of the year capable of keel and flat boat. The works of the first importance to the company, and of easy accomplishment, will be to deepen the mouths of the Sabine, Neches, Trinity and Colorado rivers, the probable cost of which will be one hundred thousand dollars, and which will, when complete, furnish from five to six thousand miles of river and canal navigation to the people of Texas.

Among the numerous improvements of which this country is susceptible, I consider a rail road of 120 miles in extent, from Copano bay, up the valley of the San Antonio to the city of Bexar, will be of immense magnitude[1]. I consider this of the first importance, not only to the interest of the company, but the prosperity of western Texas, opening at once to the coast the most rich and desirable valley the eyes of man ever saw, running directly to a spot where tradition says disease never existed, with a water power capable of supplying manufactories for a large nation, and a country around producing surer and heavier grain crops than any other known. At a future period, this road should be continued seventy miles to the valley of the San Saba, which is believed to contain more mineral wealth, in coal, iron, copper, silver and salt than is known to exist elsewhere, uniting numerous water power with all this national wealth. . .

At present there is a rail road rapidly advancing west into Louisiana; and with a connecting link of one hundred miles from Oppelousas to Sabine lake, one could pass this route from the city of Orleans to Matamoros with ease, in 70 hours. This done, and you will have nearly accomplished that great commercial desideratum, which has baffled the ingenuity of the trading world for centuries, to wit: a short road to the East Indies. You can then pass up in three days to the head of good steam boat navigation upon the Rio Grande, from whence a rail road 450 miles in length, will land you upon the Gulf of California, at the port of Guaymoos, one of the best harbors on the

---

[1]. For perspective on these proposed projects, railroad building in the United States began in 1828. The first railroad built for a regular passenger and freight traffic was the Baltimore & Ohio out of Baltimore. Ten miles of this road was opened for business in 1830. The South Carolina Railroad was begun out of Charleston in 1830 and by 1833 it had 135 miles in operation. On this road was used the first locomotive of American manufacture. [http://www.atsfrr.com/resources/welborn/spv0724.htm Accessed 10/27/2012]

Pacific, from whence (allowing me a small figure of speech) you may converse with the people of China through a speaking trumpet. I look to the time, not distant, with as much confidence, when I shall see a trip made from the Gulf of California to the city of Orleans in ten days or less, as I do to see one made from Orleans to New York in six...

I must, my dear sir, beg your indulgence for this digression—but I consider it so intimately connected with your charter privileges, it is at least sufferable. If I had an opportunity, I would call the attention of the city of Orleans to it, as she is equally interested in the work, and its accomplishment would fill the measure of her glory and grandeur. Its cost would not exceed the proposed Nashville road—To Orleans it is particularly interesting; and could the enterprise of that great city rightly understand it, she must take hold with avidity...

I might... write a volume upon the richness, beauty, and natural magnificence of Texas; upon her immense agricultural capabilities— her exhaustless mineral wealth—her grand water power for machinery, and her climate and natural productions, all of which would only aggravate your desire to have them developed, the power of doing which your charter so amply bestow...

When I have better opportunity and more time, I will take great pleasure in furnishing you many estimates and plans, which the recent improvements in railroading has just brought to light, and which will be useful to your company.

Very respectfully,

Your ob't. humble servant,

T. J. GREEN.

Thomas Green's eloquent and futuristic letter, significantly edited and shortened above, was apparently written for the purpose of soliciting investors in the Company.

Chief Justice of the Supreme Court

The same day that the charter was approved by Houston, December 16, 1836, Congress elected James Collinsworth its Chief Justice plus four associate judges. Although the Supreme Court of the Republic of Texas formally existed at this time as a branch of government, the immediate task facing the members of the court was not hearing appeals, but bringing the district court system into existence by the district judges assuming their constitutional duties as trial judges.[1] James resigned from the Senate the following day to begin his term as Chief Justice of the Supreme Court of the Republic of Texas.

---

[1]. Texas Law Review, December 1986, Vol. 65:237, p 242.

Chapter 9: Wealth and Fame at Last

As Chief Justice, James' salary of $5,000 per year was second only to the $10,000 annual salary of President Houston. Other cabinet members and officials ranged from $3,500 annually down.[1]

On December 20, 1836 John T. Collinsworth received a certificate for 3,100 shares of stock of the Texas Rail Road, Navigation and Banking Company, signed by James and three other partners. Four days later he transferred the shares to James H. Gholson for value received. He reserved the right of voting as the representative of the certificate:

---

[1]. Telegraph and Texas Register, (Columbia, TX), Vol. 1, No. 47, Ed. 1, Saturday, December 17, 1836.

On December 22, 1836 John T. Collinsworth was nominated by President Houston to the Senate for his appointment as Inspector General of the Texas Army:

Executive Department, Columbia, 22nd Dec. 1836[1]
To the Honorable Senate

Gentlemen
It affords me pleasure to make the following nominations, which with great respect I submit for the consideration of your Hon[orable] body, as well as their confirmation: For Senior Brigadier General of the Army of Texas, A. Sidney Johns[t]on; For Colonel of Ordnance, George W. Hockley; For Colonel of Engineers N. Winter Smith; For Adjutant General of the Army, E[dwin], Morehouse; For Inspector General, John T. Collinsworth;... The Gentlemen nominated are either known to me as highly meritorious or were recommended by the highest authority.

Sam Houston

The successes in James Collinsworth's two-year whirlwind life in Texas brought him to a pinnacle at the end of 1836: He had been a careful observer at the Consultation. He was an elected representative to the Convention where he was a signer of both the Declaration of Independence and the Constitution of the Republic of Texas. He was commended highly for his gallantry at the crucial Battle of San Jacinto and signed the Public and Private Treaties of Velasco. He served as commissioner to the United States, laying the groundwork for recognition of the Republic of Texas by President Jackson a few months later. He served briefly in the Senate of Texas and was elected by both houses of Congress as Chief Justice of the Supreme Court. His petition to charter the Texas Railroad, Navigation & Banking Company was passed by Congress and signed by President Houston in only three days - his one-sixteenth share in that Company would surely bring inestimable wealth and fame. The President of the Republic of Texas and the President of the United States were counted among his friends. His future could not be brighter. Or, so it seemed.

---

[1]. Amelia W. Williams and Eugene C. Barker, Eds., *Writings of Sam Houston, 1836*, (Houston: The University of Texas Press, 1938), p 521.

Chapter 10 – Good News Gives Way To Bad

Winds on the Texas plains can change in the blink of an eye. So can a man's good fortune on the frontier. Inspector General John T. Collinsworth died of congestion of the brain[1] at Fort Independence, January 30, 1837 at age 28. John's loss was a severe blow to James as it was he who had convinced John to resign his appointment in the U.S. Army to come to Texas. This letter to James Collinsworth notified him of John's death:[2]

Camp Independence

February 1st, 1837

To the Hon. James Collinsworth:
  It becomes my painful duty through this to give the intelligence of the great and irreparable misfortune that has befallen the Army as well as yourself through the dispensation of the Great Ruler of the Universe, of the death of your brother, Col. John T. Collinsworth, who died the 30th January at half past three a.m. of the congestion of the brain.
  Your brother has been in ill health from the time of his arrival at the Army but at intervals he would appear to have recovered his health and attended to the instruction of the army in drilling to the day of the departure of the President for Columbia, was unpleasant and disagreeable raining more or less during the day. Yet believing that he was sufficiently able to undergo the fatigues of a ride of eight miles to the residence of a Mr. Manifis on the Navidad where the President designed passing the night and having been solicited to accompany him, concluded to do so. On our arrival at Manifis he appeared to feel somewhat indisposed which was attributed to the cold and disagreeable evening.
  The following morning he judged that he was sufficiently well to return to camp and was anxious to return as he could obtain the more ready assistance of a physician. Accordingly, after breakfast, we left Manifis and arrived in camp without much apparent inconvenience to your brother. For some days afterwards he continued to move about, yet complaining. Dr. Fosgate, by his special request, gave him his professional attention up to the 26th of January when I called in Dr. Rogers and Reed to consult with Dr. Fosgate, and had their assistance

---

[1]. "Congestion of the Brain" was a 19th Century term used to describe many conditions including hydrocephalus, stroke, cerebral hemorrhage, meningitis, and sunstroke. Edgar Allan Poe was diagnosed as having died of congestion of the brain.

[2]. Letter from Edwin Morehouse to James Collinsworth from Camp Independence, 1 February, 1837.

and advice from that time up to his death. Every attention that was within the means of the camp was given your brother by the officers of the army.

Before I close, permit me to sympathize with you, the brother of the deceased, in the melancholy dispensation of Divine Providence which has called from us in the midst of life one who possessed that high chivalric character as a gentleman and officer-unblemished integrity and usefulness to his country.

I also enclose a copy of the proceedings of a meeting of the officers of the army paying a tribute of respect to the memory of their late worthy companion in arms.

With high respect and esteem, I am E[dwin]. Morehouse[1]

John T. Collinsworth's obituary was printed in The Houston Telegraph and Register February 21, 1837.

OBITUARY.

Colonel John T. Collinsworth, deceased, at Camp Independence on the 29th ult. Col. C. was inspector general of the Texian army. In the month of June, 1826, he entered a cadet at West Point academy, from Tennessee, of which he was a native, and graduated, with credit to himself, in 1830.

He served in the United States army until 1836, when he emigrated to Texas, and his service and personal worth called him to the station in which he died.

By service in a northern climate his constitution became impaired. He was about 27 years old. A man of the most unexceptionable habits. In a few words, he was the soldier, the gentleman, and one whose merits claimed the admiration of all who knew him. The army will deplore his loss, and reverence his memory. The soldier who falls in his prime, leaves a void in the anticipations of his friends. Thus has it been with colonel Collinsworth—the honorable, the noble, the generous—and the brave.

A glimpse of the town of Brazoria at this time plus an ominous observation regarding James' alcohol habits can be gleaned from the diary of William Fairfax Gray,[2] who had arrived recently from Virginia:

---

[1]. Original letter is in the Collinsworth file in the library of Alamo, Crockett Co. TN.

[2]. William Fairfax Gray, soldier, lawyer, and author, was born in Fairfax County, Virginia. In 1835 as land agent for Thomas Green and Albert T. Burnley of Washington, D.C., Gray visited Mississippi and Texas. Upon

Chapter 10: Good News Gives Way to Bad

Saturday, February 25, 1837.

On the Brazos.—Weather fine. Wind still ahead. The Captain took ten of the passengers in his boat and rowed us up to Brazoria, where we arrived about 4 o'clock in the afternoon. A small place, some twenty or twenty-five houses, looking decayed, dirty, uncomfortable. The seat of justice for the County of Brazoria; has been a place of some trade. Soil black, hard in dry weather, soft and tenacious when wet. Stopt [sic] at a wretched shell of a tavern, kept by Mrs. Long, widow of Colonel Long, who first settled Point Bolivar, on which she now has some claim. Her daughter, the Widow Winston, married Mr. Stiff, late of Fredericksburg, and he now lives with his mother-in-law.

Saw Judge Collinsworth, who received me very cordially, and proffered his friendship and counsel. This kindness increases my already favorable opinion of the man. His court does not sit until November. Salary, $5,000. I fear his habits will prevent his discharging the duties of his office with the credit and ability that his talents and honesty would lead the world to expect of him.[1]

Early in 1837 Chief Justice James Collinsworth and Col. Henry Millard were on the point of fighting a duel at Brazoria. Mirabeau Lamar felt "bound as a friend to both as well as a lover of truth and justice, to interpose." A correspondence between Lamar and the seconds proceeded in accord with the demands of the Code Duello, and in the end, a "court of honor" consisting of Mirabeau Lamar, General Henderson, and Colonel Hockley adjusted the difference.[2]

President Jackson Signs Resolution Acknowledging Texas Independence

Only four months after he had completed his service as commissioner to the United States, James was surely pleased that finally, at the last moment, President Jackson acknowledged the independence of Texas, as reported in the Telegraph and Texas Register:.[3]

---

arriving in Texas he attended the Convention of 1836 at Washington-on-the-Brazos and attempted but failed to obtain the position of secretary.
[1]. William Fairfax Gray, *1787-1841, From Virginia to Texas*, 1835 (Houston, Texas: Gray, Dillaye & Co., 1835-1837)
[2]. Herbert P. Gambrell, *Mirabeau Buonaparte Lamar*, (Dallas: Southwest Press, 1934), p 162.
[3]. Telegraph & Texas Register (Columbia TX) Vol. 2, No. 11, Ed. 1, March 21, 1837.

COLUMBIA, TUESDAY, MARCH 21, 1837.

We are authorised to announce that George M. Casey, late a captain in the Texas army, is a candidate for colonel of militia of this district.

Mr. John M. Shreeves is a candidate for major for the county of Brazoria.

Doctor Wm. H. Magee, formerly of Col. Fannin's regiment, is proposed by his friends as a candidate for colonel of this regiment, and will be supported by MANY VOTERS.

Extract of a letter received at the Merchants' Exchange, dated Washington, March 4th, 1837.

"The resolution to acknowledge the independence of Texas, passed the senate and house of representatives, and was signed by president Jackson on the third of March."

Alchee Labranche, Esq., speaker of the house of representatives of Louisiana, has been appointed minister to Texas.

The above intelligence is confirmed by a letter from the minister pleripotentiary at Washington city, dated the 4th instant. Gen. Hunt states that he believes the signing of this bill was the last official act of president Jackson.

The joy of our citizens occasioned by the reception of this intelligence will be heightened by the consideration, that no disparaging obstacle is now interposed which can retard the annexation.

Time may yet show to the citizens of the United States, that Travis, Fannin, and their brave associates, *fell defending the territory of their native country.*

We publish in our columns to-day the proceedings of a meeting of

Letters of Administration of John T. Collinsworth, March 27, 1837

This day came on to be heard the petition of James Collinsworth praying the court to grant to him letters of administration of succession of John T. Collinsworth deceased and a public notice having been given of said petition with citation to all parties interested in the matter to file their objections if any they had on or before this term of said Court otherwise letters would issue to the petitioner. And no objections having been filed, it is ordered, adjudged and decreed by the Court that in answer to the said petition that letters issue to the petitioner as is usual and in conformity to law.[1]

---

[1]. Republic of Texas, County of Brazoria Probate Court, March 27, 1837, p A-28.

Chapter 10: Good News Gives Way to Bad

In addition to the task of organizing the District Court system as Chief Justice, James had other important, but less significant duties to perform. On May 21, he recorded an oath by William H. Patton, Quarter Master General of the Texian Army regarding the service and death of Nathaniel M. Kerr & Joseph Kerr:

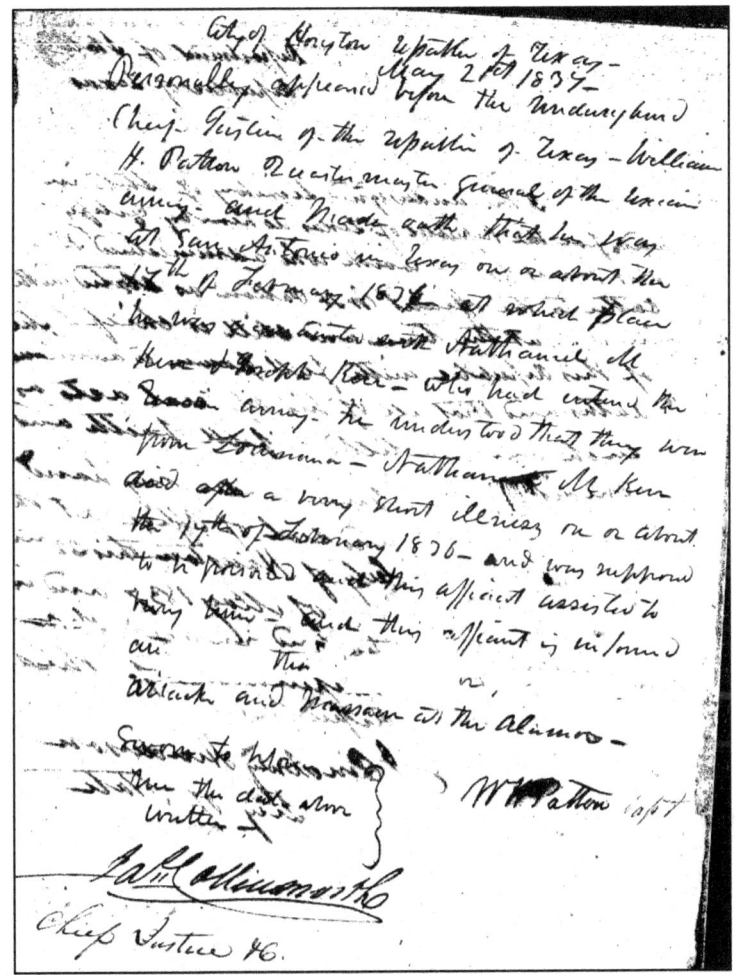

Founding of the city of Richmond Texas[1]

During the second session of the Congress of the Republic at Houston in May, 1837 Mr. Arnold, a member from Nacogdoches, offered a bill to incorporate that town which provided for a board of eight trustees and conferred general municipal powers. Some member had a clause added which required every citizen to keep a bucket, hook and ladder for use in case of fire.

Other members, impressed with Mr. Arnold's bill, added towns until the act when finally passed actually incorporated nineteen towns, among them, "the city of Houston and the town of Richmond," added by the Honorable Mosely Baker. Baker, in order to give the act real municipal flavor had the word "trustees" changed to "aldermen."

So it happened in May, 1837 "the city of Houston and the town of Richmond" were incorporated in the same act, in the same sentence, and at the motion of the same member of Congress and were off down the ages equipped with aldermen, hook and ladders and buckets. Richmond was therefore incorporated before it was begun.

The beginning of Richmond was auspicious—promoted by Colonel Robert Eden Handy, the handsomest man in Texas, with Branch T. Archer, Walter C. White, James Collinsworth, and the two Wharton's for its Godfathers and incorporated at the motion of Captain Mosely Baker. It was surveyed by that intrepid hero of San Jacinto, Moses Lapham.

An advertisement in the <u>Telegraph and Texas Register</u> on August 1, 1837 extolled the benefits of the developing town of Richmond:

PRIVATE SALE OF LOTS
IN THE
City of Richmond

"There must be towns, little and big;" and those who have the sagacity to look into the natural advantages of those offered for sale, and can see which the strong plans are will reap a great harvest; and under the increasing emigration, it will be gathered sooner than the wildest enthusiast ever dreamed of.

The proprietors now for the first time, offer to the public lots in the city of Richmond, which they will sell on accommodating terms to those who may wish to improve them. Many of the most desirable lots remain unsold, as the proprietors have refused to sell, in every instance up to this time, except under the express condition that purchasers should improve them forthwith. Five large commercial houses will be established at this place within six month viz. Walter C. White, Martin &

---

[1]. Clarence R. Wharton, *History of Fort Bend County*, (San Antonio TX, The Naylor Co. 1939), p 86.

Chapter 10: Good News Gives Way to Bad

Clow, Handy & Lusk, Texas, Masterson & Fisher, Nashville, Tenn. and James Brown & Co., New York. Various mechanical branches of business are also being established, and 'tis said' that one or two banks will be located at the city of Richmond.

The city of Richmond is situated on the west bank of the Brazos, at the foot of the great bend a short distance below the Fort Bend rapids, about 130 miles from the Gulf by water, and 65 miles by land; and is at the head of steam boat navigation, at a low stage of water. The site is on a beautiful high prairie reaching boldly to the river, and which was six feet above the highest water, during the great flood of 1833. The country from Richmond to San Antonio is connected by a chain of beautiful undulating prairies, broken only by the waters of the San Bernard, Colorado, Navidad, LaBacca and Guadalupe. On the south west, the country is open to the Gulf, and although sixty miles distant, the sea breeze is felt in all its freshness.

The best commentary upon the health of Richmond and the surrounding country is, that although by far the most densely settled portion of the republic, it never has given support to one physician. Of the quality of land, it is enough to say that the whole "Fort Bend" was taken up by "the first three hundred." When our lamented fellow citizen S. F. Austin first came to this country, he requested one of his companions, Mr. Wm. Little, who now resides near Richmond, to take a party of men and to ascend the Brazos river until he reached the best point at the head of navigation for a town. Mr. Little and his party selected the spot on which the city of Richmond is laid off; and the first settlers having forted themselves for many years at this point, gave it the well known name of "Fort Bend" "Fort settlement."

A line of steamboats will commence running from the city of Richmond to Quintana and Velasco early in autumn, to be connected with the New Orleans and Texas line of steam packets.

Robert Eden Handy,
President and Acting Treasurer.

Proprietors of the City of Richmond.

Handy & Lusk	*M'Kinney & Williams*
Martin & Clow	*Walter C. White*
Branch T. Archer	*James Collinsworth*
John A. Wharton	*Wm. H. Wharton*

While Richmond was being promoted to the citizens of Houston, funding of the Texas Railroad, Navigation and Banking Company was moving slowly. The board of directors, of which Archer was president, held a meeting in Houston, on June 30, 1837. These resolutions were reported in the Telegraph and Texas Register:[1]

> *Whereas the interests of the republic of... Texas and the Railroad, Navigation and Banking Company are intimately connected, and whereas it is desirable that the actual citizens of Texas should be stockholders in said institution: be it therefore*
>
> *Resolved, That books of subscription for stock in the Texas Rail road, Navigation and Banking Company be opened at Houston, under the direction of any two or more of the directors, on the 15th of August next [1837], and continue open until the 15th of October following, under the rules and regulations of said company: and that publication be made in the Telegraph and Texas Register printed at Houston, and in the Velasco Herald, and Nacogdoches paper for thirty days.*
>
> *Resolved, That in order to give the citizens of Texas a fair opportunity of becoming stockholders, that ten per cent only be required to be paid in at the time of subscription, in gold, silver or United States Bank bills.*
>
> *Resolved further, That for the purpose of giving the citizens generally an opportunity of subscribing, no individual shall subscribe by proxy; and no individual shall subscribe directly or indirectly for more than fifty shares of one hundred dollars each.*

These resolutions seem to indicate that the company had been unable to dispose of its stock either in the United States or to the limited monied interests of Texas.

Years later, William M. Gouge stated that the capital stock of the company was subscribed by eight individuals and firms.[2] Thomas J. Green said that there were sixteen subscribers, among whom were James H. Gholson and C. P. Green, of Virginia; William Christie, of New Orleans; James Hamilton, of South Carolina; and John Kirby Allen, Sam Houston, and himself, of Texas.[3] James' probate records showed that he owned a sixteenth share of the Company.

---

[1]. Telegraph and Texas Register, (Houston, TX), July 29, 1837, p3, col. 2.
[2]. William M. Gouge, *The Fiscal History of Texas, Embracing an Account of Its Revenues, Debts, and Currency, from the Commencement of the Revolution in 1834 to 1851-52, with Remarks on American Debts* (Philadelphia, 1852), p 61.
[3]. Reply of Gen. Thomas J. Green, to the Speech of General Sam Houston, in the Senate of the United States, August 1, 1854 (Washington, 1855), 58.

Chapter 10: Good News Gives Way to Bad

James continued his private law practice even though his governmental and corporate activities were constantly requiring his attention. Consequently, he was slow in processing his probate cases in Brazoria County TX, July Term, 1837:[1]

> It being represented to the Court that the following named persons have failed to return to the Court an estimative inventory of the estates which they respectively represent, it is ordered and decreed that a list be posted at the Courthouse door, and unless an estimative inventory is returned on or before the next regular Term of the Court, the letters of the person so failing will be revoked.

In James' list of 22 clients during this period were probate cases of two of his friends:
James Collinsworth adm. of William Arnold[2] (Ross Concession)
James Collinsworth adm. of W. J. Fannin[3]   (commander at Goliad)

Vitriolic Opposition Begins in Mid-1837

The following account of opposition to the Texas Railroad, Navigation and Banking Company comes from Herbert Pickens Gambrell's, *Anson Jones, The Last President of Texas*, except as noted:

By midyear, a vitriolic opposition had risen against the Texas Rail Road, Navigation, and Banking Company. It was Dr. Francis Moore, Jr., editor of the Telegraph and Texas Register, principal newspaper of the Republic, who led the attack. On July 29, 1837, he printed the charter of the company and wrote, in his most rhetorical style, a long editorial. The editorial concluded with a savage attack upon the wisdom and integrity of the people's representatives in Congress. He pronounced the Texas Rail Road, Navigation, and Banking a monopoly in violation of the Constitution, and served notice on July 29, 1837, that we shall oppose this corporation to the utmost extremity, and . . . shall incessantly labor to accomplish its destruction.

Moore announced that, on good authority, he had information that the company had almost finished raising the one million dollars in specie required before the bank might go into operation. His principal objection to the company was the monopoly it would possess, but doubtless he was a

---

[1]. Republic of Texas, County of Brazoria Probate Court, July Term 1837, pp 104-105.
[2]. General Arnold came to Texas in 1833 as a representative of The Ross Company. See details in Chapter 4.
[3]. James Walker Fannin was a colonel in the Texas Army in the Texas Revolution of 1835–36. His outnumbered forces surrendered to Mexicans at the Battle of Coleto Creek. Colonel Fannin and nearly all his 344 men were executed at Goliad by orders of Santa Anna.

disciple of Andrew Jackson in his opposition to banks in general, monopolistic or otherwise.

On August 12, 1837, James S. Holman, agent for the proprietors of Houston, announced that the bank was to be located in Houston and that the company had appropriated fifteen thousand dollars for the construction of a bank building. The directors had assured Holman that the bank would begin operations in November. Houstonians had subscribed $86,000, and Holman expected that within ninety days they would subscribe $214,000 more.[1]

In Brazoria County the spearhead of the anti-Texas Rail Road, Navigation, and Banking Company movement was Dr. Anson Jones, and his organ was the Matagorda Bulletin, Brazoria being at the moment without a newspaper. When Jones "chanced to see" T. J. Green's letter to Dr. Archer indiscreetly circulated to stimulate stock subscriptions he wrote a trial balloon to the editor at Matagorda on August 14, in which he pointed with pride to the uprightness of Texans outside of Congress and viewed with alarm the monster Congress had created to enslave them. He signed the letter "Franklin."

Before that letter could be published, the Telegraph and Texas Register of August 19 had announced Dr. Jones's candidacy for Congress.

In the next issue it printed a demand that the Brazoria candidates "declare their sentiments on the Rail Road, Navigation, and Banking Company."

Competition was keen for Brazoria's two seats in the House of the Second Congress. Congressman Archer, president of the Texas Rail Road, Navigation, and Banking Company, did not seek reelection, but Congressman John A. Wharton, who had failed to register a vote against the charter, announced. Mathew C. Patton, William J. Russell, Patrick C. Jack, and Anson Jones also entered the race.

John Wharton was Doctor Jones' oldest friend in Texas, a hero of San Jacinto, and dean of the Brazoria bar. He was too busy trying to rescue his brother William from the Mexicans at Matamoros to campaign. Patton was a county-seat merchant. Russell had commanded the schooner *Brazoria* in the battle of Velasco and served in the Bexar campaign, but the doctor had not yet forgiven his opposition to the Jones Resolutions for independence back in 1835. Jack had been jailed with Travis at Anahuac, served in both conventions and in the Bexar campaign, then became junior partner of Wharton & Jack, the law firm that handled the doctor's litigation.

The Matagorda Bulletin of August 23, 1837 carried the letter written by Dr. Jones but signed with the name of the Father of American Thrift:

When I first read this charter [he wrote], I rose from its perusal with astonishment . . . but . . . I did not realize the extent of the evil . . . until I chanced a few days since, by accident, to see a letter from Gen. T. J. Green [from which he quotes the most damning parts]....The famous East

---

[1]. Telegraph and Texas Register, (Houston, TX), August 12, 1837, p 3, col 1.

Chapter 10: Good News Gives Way to Bad

India Company, with its forty millions of subjects, sinks into a pigmy, in comparison with this mammoth scheme of wealth ....This paltry sum [the $25,000 bonus] will scarcely buy the slaves on a single cotton plantation, much less a whole nation of freemen! and is, comparatively, less than the miserable mess of pottage for which Esau sold his birthright. It is but a poor bait, and does not begin to cover the hook. . . . Fellow-citizens! this institution . . . will destroy, in ten thousand ways, the liberties of your country. And was it . . . to endow this splendid foreign aristocracy that you have suffered so many years of toil and privation . . . that you have so freely poured out your blood and treasure in the establishment of your independence? Was it for this you fought and bled at Velasco [Brazoria County], at Goliad, at Conception, at San Antonio, and at San Jacinto? ...Let your consciences answer these questions, and let the response be given at the polls ... September 4th, when you will be called upon to choose between the advocates and the opposers of this institution.

Anson (Franklin) Jones was elected. However, the charter became an issue in elections for the Second Congress and aroused personal antagonisms that were reflected in Texas politics for a long period of time.

In December James was certified by Sam Houston as having served in the Battle of San Jacinto.

131

Later on in December James was certified as having served in the Texian Army by Thomas J. Rusk, the former Secretary of War.

> Houston 20 Dec 1837
>
> This is to certify that Major James Collinsworth has served in the Army of Texas from the 6th day of April until the 29th day of April 1836 and acted as to the Com. g. Genl. aid de Camp, and performed the duties allotted to him at the Battle of San Jacinto with zeal for the Country and honor to himself and is hereby honorably discharged — and on the 29th of April was appointed Secy of State
>
> Tho. J. Rusk
> formerly Secy of War

Founding of the Philosophical Society[1]

On December 5, 1837, James Collinsworth was a founding member of the Philosophical Society of Texas. It was no accident that the roster of the Philosophic Society of Texas showed the names of a large number of the most prominent men in early Texas history. In the group were all the Presidents of the Republic and all of these were likewise members of the

---

[1]. Frederick Eby, *Education and Masonry in Texas to 1846*, (Waco TX: Committee on Masonic Education & Service for the Grand Lodge of Texas, A. F. and M., 1963), Introduction, pp xx-xxi.

Masonic Order. The members of these two organizations were without doubt the best informed men in Texas on the science and organization of education.

The aphorism of Francis Bacon "Knowledge is power" is probably the most frequently repeated axiom of modern times because of its pithy character and deep significance. But for simple dignity and literary brilliance two statements stand out in early Texas history as to the necessity of developing the intellectual capabilities as the prerequisite of democratic government.

The first of these introduces the Texas Declaration of Independence:
It is an axiom in political science that unless a people are educated and enlightened, it is idle to expect the continuance of civil liberty, or the capacity of self-government.
This was written, so far as can be ascertained, by James Collinsworth who was a member of the Masonic Order.

The second statement was from the eloquent mind of President Lamar in his first message to the Congress of Texas:
It is admitted by all that a cultivated mind is the guardian genius of democracy and while guided and controlled by virtue, the noblest attribute of man.
President Lamar was a member of the Masonic Order and an officer in the Philosophic Society.

Comparing the objective of the Philosophic Society with the sentiments of these two statements it is clear that they were all inspired by a conviction that the future prosperity of the infant Republic was bound up with the cultivation of all the people. The objective of the Philosophic Society was as follows:
She [Texas] calls on her intelligent and patriotic citizens to furnish to the rising generation the means of instruction within our own borders, where our children - to whose charge after all the vestal flame of Texian liberty must be committed - may be indoctrinated in sound principles and imbibed with their country's laws, love of her soil and veneration for her institutions.

Chapter 11- Death of a Dream . . . then a Man

In its April 21, 1838 issue the Telegraph and Texas Register reported, "Among the passengers who recently arrived in this city (Houston) from the U. States are Chief Justice Collinsworth, the Hon. P. C. Jack, Dr. Ashbel Smith, and Mr. [Stewart] Newel[l], consul general of the United States for Texas." Were they traveling together? Was James escorting consul general Newell promoting annexation? Was James escorting Dr. Smith, noted for his experience treating yellow fever, who had been invited by Houston to negotiate a treaty with the Comanches? We likely will never know.

Payment of the bonus required by the charter.[1]

In the spring of 1838, the Texas Railroad, Navigation & Banking Company submitted to the treasurer of the Republic twenty-five thousand dollars in Texas promissory notes as the bonus required in its charter. Henry Smith, secretary of the treasury, requested an opinion of John Birdsall, attorney general, relative to the acceptability of the promissory notes.

The 5th Section of the Bank Charter requires the Company "before going into operation, to pay to the Treasurer of Texas a Bonus, in gold or Silver, as shall be required, the sum of twenty five Thousand Dollars."

The 3d section of the act authorizing the issuing of promissory notes declares that they shall be considered as Cash, and shall be received as Cash for all dues owing or coming to the Government.

Under these provisions of the Bank charter and the promissory Note Law, the question is, does the latter dispense with the payment of the Bonus in gold or silver ...... quite a dilemma.

After constructing several paragraphs of legal argument, Birdsall came to this conclusion:

..... I am quite clear therefore that the Government is fully justified in requiring a literal compliance on the part of the Bank, with the provisions of its charter.[2]

On June 4, 1838 Birdsall sent his opinion to President Houston. With this ruling, on June 5, 1838, President Houston directed Secretary of the Treasury Smith that only gold and silver were acceptable.[3] This was the

---

[1]. Andrew Forest Muir, *The Southwestern Historical Quarterly, Vol. XLVII, APRIL, 1944, No. 4.*

[2]. Letter Book of the Treasury Department, 1836-1841 (MS. in Archives, Texas State Library), 65-67.

[3]. Letter Book of the Treasury Department, 1836-1841 (MS. in Archives, Texas State Library), p 67.

"silver" bullet tore through the spirit of James Collinsworth and sent him on his final downward spiral. The corporate existence of the Company would soon come to an end. It was, in fact, **"Too Good To Be True."**

The editor of the Telegraph and Texas Register gloated over the demise of the company in his editorial ten days after Houston's decision:

Saturday, June 16, 1838[1]

This day forms an important era in the financial history of Texas. It is enlivened by the knell of the "Texas Rail Road, Navigation and Banking Company." This person that has made as much noise in the world, and whose youth was to be constantly renewed with each generation by "golden waters," has literally perished, because the "golden drops" could not be procured in due season. It has not fallen, however, without a struggle. A few days since its few remaining friends were seen anxiously parading our streets, to gather from every quarter an amount of money sufficient to enable them to pay the bonus. They succeeded at length in raising twenty-five thousand dollars in promissory notes, with which they proceeded to the office of the Secretary of the Treasury; doubly armed with the law declaring, that the promissory notes shall "be received as cash for all dues owing of coming to the Government!" (How admirably this clause was framed to meet the occasion!) But imagine their surprise and vexation, on discovering that they had been anticipated, Sam Houston had "assumed the responsibility," and instructed the treasurer to receive nothing but "gold or silver." "Sic Semper etc.[2]*" there's Latin for them: for the Monster – "peace be to its manes."*

Presidential Campaign 1838

Presidents of the republic could not succeed themselves. Toward the end of Houston's first term as president, which would end on December 10, 1838, Mirabeau Lamar announced his candidacy. Houston supporters tried to get Rusk to run, but he refused. Also Rusk lacked two months meeting the constitutional age requirement. Houston supporters next endorsed Peter W. Grayson, the attorney general, who had worked in Washington, but on his way back to Texas Grayson committed suicide at Bean's Station in eastern Tennessee.[3]

---

[1]. Telegraph and Texas Register, (Houston, TX), Saturday, June 16, 1838.

[2]. Reference to the phrase, ***Sic semper tyrannis***. It is a Latin phrase meaning "thus always to tyrants." It is sometimes mistranslated as "death to tyrants" or "down with the tyrant."

[3]. http://www.tshaonline.org/handbook/online/articles/mzr02 Accessed 11/1/2012

Chapter 11: Death of a Dream...then a Man

After a few days of sad confusion after the death of Grayson, the Pro-Houston party came forward with a much better candidate than the late Grayson. James Collinsworth, an able lawyer from Tennessee, had served Houston in many capacities, currently as the respected chief justice of the Texas Supreme Court. He was a handsome man, a gifted speaker and an able defender of Houston's policies, for he advocated conciliation with Mexico and peace with the Cherokee. After his first successful speaking engagements, Martin Ascot and his friends agreed: 'We got ourselves a better man. Collinsworth will be our new president.'[1]

The chief justice had only two drawbacks. First, he was thirty-two years of age [not true],[2] three years shy of the constitutional requirement for president. No one in the Houston camp had bothered to check, and when troublemakers like Yancey Quimper bellowed: 'Even if he wins, he can't serve,' the Houston men replied confidently 'We'll take care of that when we get to it.'[3]

Judge Collinsworth's second impediment was a hilarious one: he was inclined to be drunk four days each week, so drunk that he could not even dress himself, and Yancey's unrelenting gang made a great deal of this, but pro Houston forces had an ingenious defense. They did not try to deny the charge; too many citizens had seen Judge Collinsworth stumbling into a tree or falling into a ditch to claim that the anti-Houston forces were defaming him. They did point out, however, that since Texas had prospered rather well under General Houston, who was drunk every morning, it was reasonable to suppose that it would do even better under Collinsworth, who would be drunk all day. As one orator shouted: 'You don't want a president who sticks his nose into everything, every day,' and this argument was so persuasive that it began to look as if the all-day-drunk Collinsworth would succeed the half-day-drunk Houston.[4]

---

[1]. James A. Michener, *Texas*, (New York: Random House, Inc., 1985), pp 489-490.

[2]. Many writers of Texas history state without proof that James Collinsworth was born in 1806, making him 32 years of age at his death. However, there are two documents that contradict that birth date. First, the minutes of the Davidson County Court in its April 1823 sessions (not 1826 as commonly stated) record that "*James Collinsworth is a man of good moral character and that he hath attained the age of twenty one years, it is ordered that he have a certificate hereof granted to him as a preparatory step to his obtaining license to practice law in this state,*" making him at least 36 at the time of his death. Second, at his death the ever-meticulous, date-oriented Masons reported that he died at age 35.

[3]. James A. Michener, *Texas*, (New York: Random House, Inc., 1985), pp 489-490.

[4]. James A. Michener, *Texas*, (New York: Random House, Inc., 1985), pp 489-490.

As one final grasp at fame, James Collinsworth announced his candidacy for President of the Republic of Texas on June 30, 1838. Only 11 days later his candidacy was announced, he was dead.

July 11, 1838: Accident, Murder or Suicide?

Absent a suicide note as Peter Grayson left when he died, historians have speculated about the cause of James Collinsworth's death. Following are quotes from several authors of Texas history quoted in earlier chapters who consider James' death as a suicide, with some mention of an accident being a possibility:

> *In 1838 he became a candidate for President of the Republic, his opponents being M. B. Lamar and Peter Grayson. A short time before the day of the election, Judge Collinsworth was drowned in Galveston Bay. It has been stated by some writers of Texas history that he deliberately threw himself from a steamer into the bay. Others tell us that he accidentally fell overboard. The preponderance of evidence favors the former account of his death.*

> *Collinsworth, in July 1838, while a candidate for the presidency against Mirabeau B. Lamar and Peter W. Grayson, committed suicide by jumping off a boat into Galveston Bay.*

> *It is ironic that Anson Jones, later to be the last president, wrote that he had expected Collinsworth's suicide because he had realized Collinsworth was going insane. Later, Jones also committed suicide.*

> *One day in late July, Judge Collinsworth, while crossing Galveston Bay on a steamer, jumped from the aft end, thus becoming the second opponent of Lamar to escape an election fight by suicide.*

> *In July 1838, Mr. Collinsworth became a candidate for President of the Republic. During* the campaign he committed suicide by jumping off a boat in Galveston Bay.

> *On July 11, however, after a week of drunkenness, he fell or jumped off a boat in Galveston Bay and drowned. Most assumed he committed suicide.*

A few accounts of his death raise the possibility of murder:

> An unattributed article printed in the <u>Evening Post</u> in Fulton, NY gave this story:
> *The Hon. James Collinsworth, Chief Justice of the Republic, was found drowned in the bay of Galveston a few days ago. The body was*

Chapter 11: Death of a Dream…then a Man

> *much mutilated and there were marks upon in which led to the belief that he had been murdered. He is said to have had considerable money with him when at Galveston. He was a man of extensive research and of superior talents. This is bad news from the young Republic and calculated to make a most unfavorable impression. The opinion already prevails to a considerable extent in this section of the Union that a large portion of the present occupants of Texas are little better than the refuse of other and more civilized countries; that rogues and murderers find a ready welcome there. A deed like that recorded above is greatly calculated to strengthen this impression. If people argue the life of the Chief Justice of the Republic cannot be considered safe from the poniard of the assassin, what peril must an ordinary citizen undergo? We trust the authorities will in this instance offer a liberal reward for the arrest of the supposed murderers and at the same time pursue all means calculated to bring them to punishment.*[1]

The family legend documented a hundred years later suggests James was murdered:

> *Uncle James and John were educated at West Point and went out West in Texas and surveyed land all through Texas and taken up land in most ever county in Texas and they made a lot of money in those days. It was not safe to travel with money and you could not send money and you could not send it like you can in these days. So he [James] started back to Tennessee with his money and was robbed and throwed [sic] into Galveston Bay.*[2]

Several reports merely contained the known facts without speculating on the cause of death. An article in the Telegraph and Texas Register[3] on July 16, five days after James's death:

---

[1]. The Evening Post, Fulton, New York Thursday Evening, August 30, 1838, quoting a letter from Texas of the 16th of July, 1838.

[2]. Recollections of Alice Elizabeth (Betty) Hill Newsom (1853-1933) written shortly before her death. The original document is in the Family Collections of Roy Newsom, Jr., 4400 Belmont Park Terrace # 154, Nashville, TN 37215.

[3]. Telegraph and Texas Register, (Houston, TX), July 16, 1838, p 1, col. 1.

> # THE TELEGRAPH.
>
> EDITED BY FRANCIS MOORE, JR.
>
> **Houston, Monday, July 16, 1838.**
>
> FOR PRESIDENT,
> ## GEN. MIRABEAU B. LAMAR.
> FOR VICE PRESIDENT,
> ## HON. DAVID G. BURNET.
>
> The Steam Boat Effort has been wrecked about forty miles east of Point Bolivar. We understand she was a very old boat, and went to pieces from the exposure to a rough sea, raised merely by a moderate breeze.
>
> The Steam Boat Warsaw arrived at Galveston from Cincinnati on Saturday last.
>
> The body of a man, so much decayed that the features could not be distinguished, was found lying on the beach of the main land, opposite Galveston, a few days since. Fears are entertained that it is the body of Judge Colinsworth.

A version of the death of James Collinsworth held by a descendant researcher holds that *"a fisherman discovered the body of a man in Galveston Bay whom he did not recognize and buried the body in a shallow grave on Tiki Island. The fisherman, upon return to Houston, reported his actions to officials. When the officials determined that James was missing they had the body exhumed, placed it in a metal casket and brought it to Houston where his body lay in state."*[1]

Author John Henry Brown provides this observation:

> *During the year 1838, Chief Justice James Collinsworth of the Supreme Court, was drowned in Galveston Bay. Some writers have*

---

[1]. Recollection of Caroline Tate recorded during a personal visit to her home by the author in 2009. She recalled she found this information in the Clayton Library in Houston, TX but could not remember the source.

Chapter 11: Death of a Dream…then a Man

repeated the mistaken story that he committed suicide. His death was a loss to the country. He was a man of superior legal ability and high mental endowments. President Houston, until the meeting of Congress, appointed John Birdsall to fill the vacancy.[1] Brown did not conjecture if the actual cause of death were accidental or murder.

So what <u>was</u> the cause of James Collinsworth's death?

First and foremost, James Collinsworth had extremely high expectations. Nothing short of fame and fortune would be acceptable. James and John no doubt had dreamed together as James painted pictures of the dazzling opportunities that lay before them, evidenced by repeated references in letters that John wrote to their sister:

April 8, 1836:

> *James informs me that there will, in all probability, be an independent government established in Texas and that he expects to be a prominent member of it and that I shall have an excellent opportunity of gaining wealth and fame and <u>he says that he has but little doubt that he will make a fortune in a short time.</u>*

June 6, 1836:

> *I have every reason to believe that I shall do much better than if I had remained in the U. S. Army and <u>that if I live and have my health I have no doubt but that I shall make a fortune</u> and from what I have learned of Texas it will be one of the most delightful climates on earth to live in as soon as the war is over, which I think will not last long.*

November 13, 1836:

> *About three or four weeks since I am now Major of Infantry and Assistant Adjutant General with the rank of major in the staff. The congress of Texas is not in session and I understand a bill has proposed the reorganization of the army and I have been assured that I should receive the commission of Colonel.*
> *I presume that I shall enjoy my health as well here as in the states after I become acclimated. And I am convinced that I can do better here than in any part of the States. <u>If I live and have my health I feel certain of making a fortune here, and I shall, I think, certainly gain as much fame as I should in my mother country</u> and besides this country may and, I think it probably will,*

---

[1]. John Henry Brown, *History of Texas from 1685 to-1892*, Volume 2, p 140.

be one of the United States before very long and then the state of Texas will be considered the choice state of all the southern states.

Secondly, James was deeply in debt and had severe cash flow issues. He was a full time public servant with a part-time law practice. Did he spend his money on liquor? Definitely, way too much. However, he did not have much income to spend:

Soon after San Jacinto, on May 13, 1836, after fifteen months in Texas he wrote President Burnet, "…the result however has been to bring upon me considerable pecuniary loss at home [Nashville] and absolute indigence here [Texas], having expended what little of means I brought with me and accumulated some debts without having ever called or received one cent in any way whatever or one acre of land from the government…"

James had been commissioner to the United States from May to November, 1836 yet his payment of $3,000 was approved by an act of congress more than a year afterwards.

He became Chief Justice on December 16, 1836 yet did not receive his first salary payment until November 5, 1837, almost a year in arrears.

Even though his salary was second highest in the Texas government, it would have taken three plus years' salary to pay his creditors.

Thirdly, the public escapades of drunkenness described earlier provide ample proof that James was addicted to alcohol, and may have been before he left Nashville. Several of his friends, also quoted in earlier chapters, had made recent remarks about his struggles with addiction:

Henderson King Yoakum, contemporary historian: *"He had emigrated to Texas to rid himself of a false habit, which unfortunately pursued him, and brought him to a premature grave."*

William Fairfax Gray, soldier, lawyer and author: *"I fear his habits will prevent his discharging the duties of his office with the credit and ability that his talents and honesty would lead the world to expect of him."*

Anson Jones, then Minister to the United States: "*I had expected it [James' death] as I knew him to be deranged, and when excited by liquor, almost mad.*"

This combination of high expectations, severe indebtedness and addiction to alcohol was a bomb ready for ignition. Sadly, bad news is very difficult for an alcoholic to process. Each rejection, each disappointment, each failure requires more and more alcohol to dull the pain and hide the depression.

The swirling tornado of bad news started when John, the 28-year-old colonel-to-be, died from a fever brought from Wisconsin or caught en route

Chapter 11: Death of a Dream...then a Man

to Texas. In either case James sure regretted his insistence that John come to Texas.

Then came the "panic of 1837" in the United States and Texas which contributed to insufficient funding of the Texas Railroad, Navigation & Banking Company. In addition, there were vicious attacks on the Company and some of James' associates in government by the newspaper and a few men whom he had considered friends.

And when his friend Houston, who, on basis of an opinion by the Attorney General, had to require payment in gold or silver from the cash-poor Company, there would not have been enough pain-relieving whiskey and brandy in the barrels he had destroyed a few years back to relieve his pain. He could no longer face himself and his friends – no doubt he took his own life.

The Funeral

A special meeting of Temple Lodge, No. 4, Ancient York Masons, held at the Senate Chamber, in the City of Houston, on Sunday morning, the 22d July, A.D. 1838, A.L. 5838...The Lodge was opened in the Master Mason's Degree, in due and ancient form. The object of the meeting was stated by the Worshipful Master to be, to pay the funeral Masonic honors over the remains of our worthy and beloved Brother, James Collinsworth. Bro. Collinsworth, at the time of his decease, was Chief-Justice of the Republic of Texas, and a member of Holland Lodge...The Lodge was organized in ancient and solemn form, to perform the last honors over the remains of our worthy departed Brother of Holland Lodge, No. 1...The fraternity then moved with the procession to the Capitol, where the corpse was deposited, and listened to an eloquent eulogy pronounced by our worthy fellow-citizen, A. M. Tompkins[1], Esq., preceded by a few pertinent remarks from Bro. Lawrence, officer of the day. The procession was again formed, and proceeded to the graveyard of the City of Houston, where the remains of Bro. Collinsworth were deposited with solemn and Masonic prayers, ceremonies, and honors.[2]

James Collinsworth Death Notice, July 28, 1838

> *The funeral of the late Chief Justice James Collinsworth took place on Tuesday last. An oration was delivered on the occasion by A. M. Thompkins, Esq. The remains were followed to the grave by a large*

---

[1]. Augustus M Tompkins was a member of the bar and District Attorney of Harris County (Houston).

[2]. Freemasons. Texas. Grand Lodge.. Proceedings of the Grand lodge of Texas, from its organization in city of Houston, Dec. A.D. 1837, A.L. 5837, to the close of the grand annual communication held at Palestine, January 19, A.D. 1857, Vol. 1, Book, 1857, p 37.

concourse of our citizens, including the Masonic fraternity of this community.[1]

The Results of the Election of 1838

Mirabeau Lamar took his campaign seriously. He promised to rectify the "blunders" of Houston's administration, and won by a vote of 6,995 to 252 over Senator Robert Wilson. David Burnet was elected vice president.

The Texas News, Houston, September 10, 1838 reports the election results with a political jab:

The friends of President Sam Houston have taken some pleasure during the last week in pointing out that President-elect Mirabeau B. Lamar won his great victory over two dead men and a nonentity. It is almost correct to say that Lamar actually did win by default. During the campaign Chief Justice James Collinsworth committed suicide by jumping from a steamer into Galveston Bay and Peter Grayson took his own life in a tavern in Tennessee. The developments left only Lamar and "Honest Bob" Wilson in the race. Lamar won by a vote of 6,695 to 252.[2]

---

[1]. Telegraph and Texas Register, (Houston, TX), Vol. 3, No. 48, Ed. 1, Saturday, July 28, 1838.

[2]. Ralph W. Steen, Editor, The Texas News, (Austin: The Steck Company), p 65.

Chapter 12 - Probate Reveals an Insolvent Estate

August 14, 1838 - Letters of Administration[1]

This day was heard the petition of T. F. McKinney praying for letters of administration on the estate of James Collinsworth dec'd, and public notice thereof having been given according to law, Edwin Waller appeared by his attorney and filed his objections to the petition of said McKinney. And the Court having heard the arguments of counsel on both sides and duly weighed the evidence, it is ordered adjudged and decreed that the said Thomas F. McKinney be appointed administrator and that letters issued to him as customary on his giving bond and security. Whereupon the said T. F. McKinney filed his petition praying that an inventory be taken of said property, that a curator be appointed for the absent heirs and that the perishable property of said estate be sold.

It was then ordered, adjudged and decreed by the Court that the prayer of the petition be granted that in order for inventory and appraisement issue and that Robert J. Townes[2] be appointed curator for the absent heirs and that the perishable property be sold at the Court house door in the town of Brazoria for cash after giving 10 days notice to that effect.

September 4, 1838 - Estimative Inventory of the Books.[3]

We the undersigned appraisers appointed by the Hon. Wm. J. Scott to make an estimative inventory of the books of James Collinsworth, dec'd, do appraise the same as follows, to wit,

# Vol	Author/Title	
2	British Eloquenses	$2.00
1	Clarks _____ (_____)	2.00
1	Treatise on Anatomy	1.00
1	Ferguson on Anatomy	1.00
1	Elements of _____	1.00
1	Hermans Poems	.50
1	History of Tennessee	1.00
1	Treatise on Mechanics	1.00
1	Davis on Surveying	1.50
1	_____ Works	2.00
1	_____ _____	1.00

---

[1]. Republic of Texas, County of Brazoria Probate Court, August 14, 1838, Book B, p 58.
[2]. Robert J. Townes (1806-1860) was a judge and Texas Secretary of State.
[3]. Republic of Texas, County of Brazoria Probate Court, September 4, 1838, Book A, pp 172-174.

1	American Geography	1.00
1	Grammers Surveying	1.50
1	Bridges Mechanics	1.50
2	Science of War	3.00
1	Bucks Theological Dictionary	1.50
3	French Dictionary	5.00
1	French Dictionary	1.00
1	Ainsworth's Latin Dictionary	3.00
1	Mathis Dictionary	2.00
2	Spanish Dictionary	5.00
2	Worchester Gazetteer	8.00
1	Clarks _____	.50
1	Infantry Tactics	1.00
23	British Poets 2 volumes missing	25.00
1	Moore's Power on ____ ____	5.00
1	History of Charles XII	.50
1	Gil Blas (incomplete)	1.00
1	Masonic Charts	1.00
1	Historic _____	.50
1	_____ _____	.25
1	Family Cabinet attys	2.00
1	Watts Logic	.75
1	Greek Grammar	1.00
1	_____ Arithmetic	.50
1	Trigonometry	.50
2	_____ _____	1.00
1	Harpers _____	.25
1	Lacroix French	2.00
1	_____ Geometric _____	2.00
1	Rush on the Mind	1.00
1	Woods Law of Nations	3.00
3	Marshmonts Papers	3.00
1	Formans Optics	1.00
1	Wept of the Wish-Ton-Wish	.25
1	Tables of Logarithms___ (Treasch)	2.00
2	Shakespeare	4.00
4	Eloquenses of ___ (1 vol. missing)	5.00
2	Websters 9th Dictionary	20.00
10	Montworth on Pleadings	25.00
1	Laws of Tennessee	1.00
1	Hall on Libels	2.50
1	Fields Blackstone	.50
1	Powels on _____	5.00
2	American Jurist	4.00
1	Boscowan on Penal Statutes	1.00
3	Easts _____ Laws (incomplete)	10.00

Chapter 12: Probate Reveals an Insolvent Estate

2	Fonlelasigues Equity	10.00
1	Remmington on _____	2.00
1	Masters Law of Nations	2.00
1	Pleas of the Crown (French)	1.50
1	_____ Book	1.00
1	Kyd on Bills	1.00
2	Harris on Chancery	5.00
4	_____ Reports	10.00
4	Condensed Chancery Reports	20.00
1	Pecks Reports	1.00
2	Wheatons _____	10.00
1	Powels on Mortgages	5.00
3	Cruise on Real Property	12.00
1	Sugdens Law of Vendors	5.00
2	Chitty on Pleadings (incomplete)	5.00
1	Stephan on Pleadings	3.00
3	Stones _____ Laws on the Constitution	15.00
3	Laws of the W. L.	9.00
1	Mortgage on Set Off	1.00
1	Russels Chancery Report (incomplete)	3.00
1	Russels on Crimes (incomplete)	3.00
3	Cokes Institutions	10.00
1	Christies Digest	2.00
4	Chittys Criminal Law	20.00
1	Chitty on Bills	7.50
1	Livingston Penal Law	20.00
1	Elliots American Diplomatic Code (incomplete)	5.00
1	Kent Commentary (incomplete)	5.00
2	Portedas (English)	10.00
2	Cormats Civil Law	20.00
1	Starke on Evidence	15.00
1	Civil Code of Louisiana	10.00
1	Code of _____	10.00

In testimony whereof we have hereto ___ ___ our hands this 4 day of September 1838.

      Thomas Blackwell
      A.C. Hyde

Sworn to and subscribed
Before me at office
Edward Pursell
Dist Clerk

September 14, 1838 - Additional Inventory of the Estate of James Collinsworth, dec'd.[1]

1 Negro man named Morris	$1000-
1 horse	300-
1 shot gun	10-
Filed 14 Sept. 1838 Total	$1310-

October 23, 1838 - Supplementary Inventory of the Estate of James Collinsworth, dec'd.[2] *This trunk likely had belonged to his brother John.*

1	leather trunk	$12.00
	Articles in trunk	
1	Cooper & Thompson in 1 vol.	5.00
1	military coat old	3.00
1	old blue coat	5.00
1	plume	.25
1	military cap	1.00
1	set epaulets	25.00
1	pair gold spectacles	15.00
1	pair military pants	6.00
1	lot shirt collars & bosoms & two shirts	4.00
1	military coat	40.00
1	old coat	5.00
6	old vests	6.00
1	Bowie knife	15.00
		142.25

Filed 23 October 1838
R.I. Colder
Thomas Blackwell

August 26, 1839 - Court Grants Disposition of Part of Assets.[3]

This day came on to be heard the petition of Thos. J. McKinney admin. of the estate of James Collinsworth dec'd, representing that twelve months have passed since letters were granted him upon said estate and that he is unable at this time to make a final settlement of the same, that the debts

---

[1]. Republic of Texas, County of Brazoria, Probate Court September 14, 1838, Book A, p 174.
[2]. Republic of Texas, County of Brazoria Probate Court, October 23, 1838, Book A, p 174.
[3]. Republic of Texas, County of Brazoria Probate Court, August 26, 1839, Book B, pp 155-156.

against exceed the assets in his hands and that it will be required to sell a portion of the property belonging to the estate, presenting to the Court a statement of his account with the estate and praying for an order of Court to sell for cash a negro man called Morris and lots No. five and six in Block No. 48 in the town of Quintana and the Court having considered the matter it is ordered, adjudged and decreed that the prayer of the petition be granted and that the before mentioned property be sold for cash.

September 18, 1839 – McKinney Petitions Court To Collect a Debt.[1]

Republic of Texas
County of Brazoria

To the Honorable judge of the second judicial district of the Republic of Texas. The petition of Thomas F. McKinney administrator in the succession of James Collinsworth, deceased, respectfully represents that Warren D. C. Hall of said county, is indebted to said succession in the sum of one thousand dollars besides interest: for that the said Hall on the 4th day of December 1837, made his certain promissory note by which he promised twelve months after the date thereof, to pay James Collinsworth in _____ one thousand dollars for value received but which debt the said Hall refuses to pay.

The petitioner therefore prays that the said Hall may be cited to appear before the next term of the court for said county and answer this demand, and that he be commanded to pay said debt with interest & costs and for _____ this atty.
Sept. 18, 1839.

December 30, 1839 – Petition for Title for Land Previously Sold.[2]

This day came on to be heard the petition of Robert Wilson that James Collinsworth now deceased, on the 30th day of November 1837 assigned conveyed and released to the petitioner all his right, title and interest to Lots nine and ten in Block thirty-three in the town of Houston and that the conveyance was informal and praying for a decree of the court to compel Thos. J. McKinney, admin. of the succession of said James Collinsworth, to make to him a title for the said lots. And the court having heard the parties by their counsel and being satisfied of the truth of the allegations in the petition contained, it is ordered, adjudged and decreed that the said T. F. McKinney make to the said Robert Wilson a deed to the said lots as prayed for.

---

[1]. Republic of Texas, County of Brazoria District Court, August 26, 1839, District Clerks Office.

[2]. Republic of Texas, County of Brazoria Probate Court, December 30, 1839, Book C, p10.

December 30, 1839 - Court Grants Sale of Stock in Texas Railroad, Navigation and Banking Co.[1]

This day came on to be heard the petition of Thos. F. McKinney administrator of the estate of James Collinsworth dec'd, representing that the said estate is insolvent and that it will be necessary to sell all the property belonging to said estate to pay the debts thereof and praying for an order of Court to sell the interest of said succession in and to the Texas Railroad, Navigation and Banking Company consisting of one-sixteenth of the stock thereof and that the same be sold according to law for cash, and the Court having considered the matter and read the petition and being satisfied of the truth of the allegations therein contained, it is ordered, adjudged and decreed that the prayer of the petition be granted and that said stock as aforesaid be sold as prayed.

February 9, 1840 - **Telegraph and Texas Register** Notice of Claims Against the Estate[2]

NOTICE

THE undersigned will at the next Probate Court of Brazoria County, present his account as administrator of the estate of James Collinsworth, deceased. All persons having claims against the estate are requested to present them duly authenticated; and all persons interested are hereby notified to attend and except to the account and tableau of distribution if they think proper to do so.

Thos. F. McKinney,
Adm'r. J. Collinsworth
February 9, 1840

October 29, 1840 – District Court Orders Collection of Debt from Estate of Thomas J. Green.[3]

A formal court order was issued by the District Court of Brazoria County to the sheriff of said county to levy and collect from the estate of Thomas J. Green thirty four dollars and twenty four cents against the estate of Thomas

---

[1]. Republic of Texas, County of Brazoria Probate Court, December 30, 1839, Book C, p18.
[2]. Brazos Courier, (Brazoria, TX.), Vol. 2, No. 10, Ed. 1, Tuesday, April 21, 1840.
[3]. Republic of Texas, County of Brazoria District Court, October 29, 1840, District Clerks Office.

Chapter 12: Probate Reveals an Insolvent Estate

J. Green that he owed to James Collinsworth for Collinsworth representing him in a case before Collinsworth died. Green is also dead. The recovery was made on the 29th of October 1840 and this order was not issued until the 14 of April in 1841.

Inventory of the Contents of Two Trunks Belonging to the Estate[1]

Note: The date of this inventory is not known; it is filed between 5/11/1839 and 11/2/1841.

1   W.P. Austin's deed for 10 shares in the Town of Liverpool.
2   W.P. Austin's deed for 4 lots in same.
3   Thomas J Green receipt for one thousand dollars paid on a/c his share in the Railroad Bank $1000.
4   Power of Attorney from A.M. Williamson to review his quarter pay $750 due 20th June by Govt. of Texas $750.
5   B.T. Archer G.H. Stines 2 notes favor Thomas J. Green 12 ____ Dec 24, __ $5000.
6   Certificate for 3126 shares in the Railroad Bank.
7   Due Bill of R. Picken $5.00
8   Due Bill of M. Davis $25.00
9   Receipt of W. Parson for 2 notes for collection $390.00
10   _____ $10.00
11   J. Murphy note $10.
12   John Gilbert $50.00
13   P.W. Grayson receipt for _____ note $500.00
14   Grayson and Bardwell note $200.00
15   W.D.C. Hall note Dec 4, 1837 $1000.00
16   N. Sylvester note $250.00
17   Jno. Gordon note $250.00
18   M.E.C. Johnson $350.00
19   45 Certificates for lots in the Town of Kennard, TX

Other inventory

1   double barrel gun
1   horse
2   saddle and bridle
1   blanket
1   negro man Morris
6   vests, 1 uniform coat and 2 pr pants
1   uniform _____ coat
2   cloth dress coats

---

[1]. Republic of Texas, County of Brazoria Probate Court, ca. December 30, 1839, Book A, pp 303-304.

2 cotton and linen shirts
1 bosom and 5 linen collars
1 box epaulets
2 books
1 knife
1 pair gold spectacles
  Laws of Texas
  Ink Stand
  Cap and plume
2 trunks

We the _____ having been prescribed to take an inventory of two trunks containing sundry _____ belonging to the estate of James Collinsworth deceased, also of his property in this place and have examined and found therein as stated.

                James _____

June 26, 1843 - Final Settlement of the Estate of James Collinsworth[1]

This day came on to be heard the petition of Thomas F. McKinney administrator of the estate of James Collinsworth, deceased, praying that he may be allowed to settle his account as said administrator and due notice having been given and the account being now reported for settlement and allowance. It is hereby ordered, adjudged and decreed that the account be and the same is hereby allowed and approved, that the claims exhibited against the estate and allowed by the administrator, a schedule of which accompanies the petition, be and the same is hereby approved, that the sum of one thousand & seventy nine dollars and eighty six cents in the hands of the administrator, be by him paid to the creditors in proportion to the amount of their respective claims and according to the tableau of distribution filed with the account, and that the sales made by the administrator be and the same are hereby confirmed, and that the clerk to make a complete record of all the papers here exhibited and produced to the Court, all of which is ordered adjudged and decreed by the Court.

---

[1]. Republic of Texas, County of Brazoria Probate Court, June 26, 1843, Book D, pp 35-36.

Chapter 12: Probate Reveals an Insolvent Estate

	Schedule of Probate Costs	
Date	To or For	Amount
1838	To cash paid clerk's fee	$162.57
1838	To cash paid clerk's fee	$72.38
1838	To cash Judge of Probate	$150.00
1838	To cash ? for printing	$30.00
1838	To cash Jacks and Townes attys	$1,040.75
1838	To cash Ledger of Thompson for Printing	$15.00
Jany 1843	To Amount of my account herewith	$222.78
Jany 1843	To Commission on ? @ 5%	$240.70
1840	To Commission on ?	$240.71
Jany 1	To cash pd L D Jones % proceeds Sale of Property in Quintana	$1,000.00
Jany 1	Cash received T.J. Green ? ? ?	$135.30
Feb 18 43	Pd R.J. Townes for two judgement fees of Houston 1 ? 1?	$313.78
	Chief Justice Fee	$10.00
		$3,633.97
	Schedule of Collections	
Date	From or For	Amount
1838	By Amt collected from A.G.C. Johnson	$95.85
	By Amt on horse at probate sale	$200.00
	By Amt Boy Morris	$1,200.00
	By Amt sale of books	$249.75
	By Amt Wm. H. Jack note due	$200.00
	By Amt quit claim against Johnson	$279.65
	By Amt quit claim against W.D.C. Hall with interest	$236.50
	By Amt proceeds Sale of property in Quintana	$1,000.00
1843		$1,079.51
		$4,541.26

Schedule of Debts Exhibited Against the Estate and Allowance by the Administrator							
Creditor	When done	Status of Claim	Rate of Interest	Principal	Interest	Total	Share
1 McKinney & Williams	Jany 43	ap		$5,521.15	$160.00	$5,770.00	$403.97
2 T J Green	Jun 24 37	Judgmnt	5%	$5,000.00	$1,500.00	$6,500.00	$455.00
3 T H Everett	June 4 38	note	10%	$1,000.00		$1,505.54	$103.38
4 B C Franklin	Dec 29 37	note	5%	$120.00		$155.00	$10.71
5 Jno A Huston	Oct 38	ap		$13.54		$15.80	$1.14
6 Wm H McGee	June 38	ap		$25.00		$21.25	$2.18
7 Wm H McGee	June 37	ap		$199.50	$59.02	$259.12	$18.15
8 A Lynch	July 37	ap		$30.00		$39.00	$2.73
9 ?	Jany 37	ap		$15.00		$20.15	$1.14
10 Joshua Sharp	Jany 37	ap		$104.00		$117.00	$8.17
11 Geo W Hockley	Dec 39	ap		$35.50		$65.19	$4.55
12 ? Co.	Aug 37	ap		$5.00		$7.45	$0.54
13 ?	Jany 38	ap		$65.50		$80.21	$5.60
14 G B McKinsty	Mch 37	ap		$20.00		$26.25	$1.53
15 James Long	Mch 37	ap		$173.12		$227.18	$15.89
16 Waller & Masterson	June 38	ap		$148.75		$185.90	$13.01
17 P C Jack	April 38	ap		$123.00		$159.47	$10.83
18 ?	Feby 39	ap		$8.50		$10.20	$0.41
19 J N Reed	Oct 38	ap		$58.50		$48.48	$4.88
				$12,666.06		$15,213.19	$1,063.81

There was no evidence in the probate records that these land grants were included in the estate.

Name	File	Acres	Comment
James Collinsworth	001693		Court of Claims
James Collinsworth	000001		Brazoria Co. Clerk Returns
James Collingsworth	000516	640	Archer Co.
James Collingsworth	000909	1476.13	Wilbarger Co.

Chapter 13 - In Memoriam

When the account of Judge Collinsworth's death reached the people, real sorrow was felt. His opponent in the race for President of the Republic, Mr. Lamar, said: "I regret to learn of Judge Collinsworth's tragic death. He possessed a wonderfully bright intellect and was a most useful citizen." Thomas J. Rusk said: "He was a brave soldier, strong friend and a great lawyer. His wise counsel will be missed."[1]

The editors of the New Orleans Commercial Bulletin have received Texas Papers to the 20th ult. Things remained quiet, and no important event had transpired in the country. The newspapers were chiefly occupied in canvassing the merits of the respective candidates for the presidency and vice presidency. The death of the Hon. James Collingsworth, chief justice of Texas, is mentioned. The bar had a meeting at Houston, to express their esteem for his character, and regret for the bereavement the public sustained by his decease.[2]

Judge James Collinsworth's short residence in Texas was marked by great usefulness to the Republic. Mr. Yoakum, the historian, described Judge Collinsworth as a "man of fine talent and great urbanity. He had a pleasant wit and was a most admirable companion and of scrupulous integrity."[3]

At an address before the Texas Bar Association at Galveston in 1895 Judge W. W. Terrell said this of Judge Collinsworth:

> *"Judge James Collinsworth left a record of which we should all be proud. He was a lawyer of distinguished ability who preferred to settle his clients' troubles out of court where it was possible. He despised long drawn out litigation. Judge Thomas Rusk once told me that Judge Collinsworth possesses the brightest legal mind he had ever encountered at the bar; that he would never rest his cases on technicalities, but depended on the law's intent to win his cause. 'His interpretation of the law's meaning,' said Judge Rusk, was clear, logical and convincing; and his persuasive argument before the*

---

[1]. Sam Houston Dixon, *The Men Who Made Texas Free*, (Houston: Texas Historical Society), p 116-117.

[2]. Wm. Ogden Niles, *Niles National Register,* Vol. 54, Wm. Ogden Niles, Washington, 1838, p 355.

[3]. Sam Houston Dixon, *The Men Who Made Texas Free*, (Houston: Texas Historical Society), p 115.

> *court convinced judge and jury of the correctness of his views. The younger lawyers dreaded to meet him before the bar as an opponent, although he was very considerate of their feeling and often aided them in presenting their pleas. His success was not due so much to his eloquence as his familiarity with every phase of legal construction. His mind was a storehouse of legal opinions and his knowledge of common law practice was marvelous.*[1]

In presenting a portrait of Chief Justice James Collinsworth to the Supreme Court of the State of Texas, Floride Peterson compared James Collinsworth to George Washington: "Washington, it is said, was childless that he may be called the father of his country. So, it may be said, Collinsworth never wrote an opinion that he may be called the father of our judiciary."[2]

When a group of counties were created from the Young Land District in 1876 by an act of the legislature, one of them was named for James Collinsworth, "a signer of the Declaration of Independence and first Chief Justice of the Supreme Court of the Republic of Texas."[3] Sadly, the act contained a misspelling of his name; the panhandle county today is known as Collingsworth County. Its population in 1880 was 6 and 357 in 1890. In 1900 the census reported 1,233 inhabitants and 5,224 in 1910.

James Collinsworth has been much honored by the State of Texas, as have the other important men of the period of the Republic. His name is inscribed on the Wall of Honor in the San Jacinto Monument, on a Historical Marker at Washington-on-the-Brazos and the Hall of State in Dallas. A street in Houston is named for him.

In 1931 funds were appropriated for several founders of the Republic of Texas and on August 15, 1931 a monument bearing the seal of the state of Texas was erected near his burial in the old City Cemetery, now Founders Memorial Park in Houston. It is inscribed as follows:

---

[1]. Sam Houston Dixon, *The Men Who Made Texas Free*, (Houston: Texas Historical Society), p 117.

[2]. Texas Law Review, December 1986, Vol. 65:305, p 308.

[3]. Sam Houston Dixon and Louis Wiltz Kemp, *The Heroes of San Jacinto*, (Houston: The Anson Jones Press, 1932), p 46.

Chapter 13: In Memoriam

Front:
Born in Tennessee, 1806; Drowned in Galveston, July 11, 1838, and his remains brought by boat up Buffalo Bayou to Houston; His remains interred in this cemetery under the auspices of Temple Lodge No. 4; First Masonic Funeral ever held in Texas.

Back:
Delegate to the Consultation held at San Felipe, 1835; signer, from Brazoria Municipality, of the Texas Declaration of Independence; "Bore himself as a Chief" at San Jacinto; Secretary of State, 1836; Senator in the Congress of Texas, 1836; First Chief Justice of the Supreme Court of Texas; a county in Texas was named in his honor.

Index

Adams: John Quincy, 13, 19
Alamo, 59, 61, 65, 66, 70, 71, 74, 77, 85, 86, 122
Allen: John Kirby, 128
Almonte: Don Juan, 85
Alston: Willis, 14, 15
Archer: Branch T., 101, 102, 110, 111, 112, 114, 115, 126, 127, 128, 130, 151, 154
Arnold: William, 44, 129
Ascot: Martin, 137
Austin: Stephen F., 95, 101, 102, 111, 112, 113, 114, 115
Bacon: Francis, 133
Baker: Mosely, 126
Baltimore, 44, 99, 117
Battle of Gonzales, 55
Battle of New Orleans, 8
Battle of San Jacinto, v, 81, 86, 87, 89, 93, 95, 101, 120, 131
Bell: John, 11, 34, 42, 46
Bennett: Joseph L., 69, 84
Birdsall: John, 135, 141
Bowie: Jim, 59, 70, 148
Brazoria, 35, 44, 45, 52, 53, 54, 57, 58, 62, 78, 81, 87, 102, 103, 109, 112, 122, 123, 124, 129, 130, 131, 145, 148, 149, 150, 151, 152, 154, 157
Brazos, 53, 54, 57, 62, 66, 67, 73, 74, 75, 81, 112, 114, 122, 123, 127, 150, 156
Brigham: Asa, 58
Bryan: Moses Austin, 86
Buffalo Bayou, 81, 82, 83, 88, 157
Bunton: J. W., 114
Burleson: Edward, 84
Burnet: David G., 72, 73, 74, 81, 86, 87, 88, 90, 91, 95, 97, 99, 101, 110, 113, 142, 144
Byrom: John S. D., 58, 62
Calhoun: John C., 19, 73, 96
Carson: Samuel P., 70, 72

Chickasaw Treaty, 39
Childress: George C., 63, 66, 70, 77, 92
Christie: William, 128
Clay: Henry, 9, 13, 14
Clover Bottom, 13
Cobbs: Robert L., 28, 29
Cockrill: John, 1, 2; Mark, 9
Coffee: John, 8, 28, 40, 41
Coleman: Robert, 86
Collins: Aristarcus, 9
Collinsworth: Alice Thompson, 3, 9, 18; Benjamin Franklin, vi, 7, 8, 9, 10, 13, 14, 79; David, 1; David Cook, 53, 55, 79; Edmund, 1, 2, 7, 8, 9, 13; Elizabeth Catherine, 7, 8, 9; George Morse, 53, 55, 56, 79, 97; George Washington, 8, 35, 42, 45, 46, 51, 53, 79, 97; John, 2; John Thompson, 7, 8, 14, 35, 78, 79, 96, 97, 100, 102, 105, 107, 119, 120, 121, 122, 124; Parmelia Ann, 7, 8, 9, 10, 78, 96, 105; Susan Eliza, 7, 8, 9
Columbia, 56, 57, 99, 101, 104, 109
Corrupt Bargain, 14
Cos: Martin Perfecto, 54, 59, 84
Craighead: David, 25, 27, 29; Thomas, 26
Crawford: William Harris, 13
Crockett: David, 59
Crutcher: Thomas, 25, 29
Cumberland Compact, 4
Currin: R. P., 39
Davis: Loyd, 13, 46, 51, 97, 106; Parmelia Ann Collinsworth, 46, 51
De Morse: Charles, 101
Donelson: Andrew Jackson, 9, 14; John, 3, 4
Dozier: James I., 36, 37

duel, 15, 18, 102, 123
Dyer: Robert, 8, 44
Eaton: John H., 40
Ellis: Richard, 62, 66, 71, 77
Emuckfau, 8
Everett: Edward, 40; Stephen H., 62, 109
Fannin: James W., 53, 55, 70, 73, 129
Farris: Willis A., 63
Fisher: John, 66
Fletcher: Thomas, 12, 21, 30, 31, 34
Forsyth: John, 98, 99, 103
Fort Winnebago, 35, 78, 96
Foster: Ephraim Hubbard, 24
Fox: Barbara, 1
Franklin: Benjamin C., 57, 87
Gaines: James, 66; Pendelton, 82
Galveston, 66, 81, 88, 114, 138, 139, 140, 144, 155, 157
Gazley: Thomas J., 62, 63, 70
Gholson: James H., 119, 128
Goliad, 55, 67, 70, 73, 85, 86, 129, 131
Gonzales, 54, 55, 59, 66, 70, 72, 112, 113
Goodrich: Benjamin B., 29, 63, 70, 75
Graham: William A., 14
Gray: William Fairfax, 102, 122, 123, 142
Grayson: Peter W., 88, 90, 95, 96, 97, 98, 99, 102, 103, 136, 138, 144
Green: C. P., 128; Thomas J., 90, 110, 115, 118, 122, 128, 130, 150, 151
Groce: Jared E., 73
Grundy: Felix, 13, 24, 27, 31, 32, 51; James P. H., 51
Hall: D. C., 149, 151; Lindsey C., 11
Hamilton: James, 128; Robert, 63, 70, 77
Handy: Robert Eden, 126, 127

Hardeman: Bailey, 63, 68, 72, 88, 90
Harrisburg, 74, 81, 82, 83, 84
Henderson: James Pinckney, 37, 90, 111, 113, 123
Hermitage, 9, 98, 100, 103
Hill: John, 13
Hockley: George W., 68, 83, 84, 85, 120, 123
Holland Masonic Lodge, 58, 143
Holman: James S., 130
Houston: Sam, 12, 13, 14, 44, 62, 63, 65, 66, 67, 70, 72, 73, 74, 75, 76, 78, 81, 82, 84, 85, 86, 87, 88, 95, 101, 103, 105, 109, 113, 114, 119, 120, 128, 131, 135, 136, 137, 141, 143, 144, 155, 156
Hunt: Memucan, 90
Inaugural Ball, 19, 20
Independence: (ship), 88, 96, 102
Indians: Cherokee, 5, 67, 137; Chickasaw, 39, 40, 41; Choctaw, 40; Comanche, 67, 135; Creek, 4, 7, 8, 67
Invincible: (ship), 90
Jack: Patrick C., 130, 135; William H., 99; William J., 95
Jackson: Andrew, 8, 12, 13, 18, 19, 21, 22, 23, 24, 26, 27, 28, 30, 31, 34, 37, 39, 40, 41, 42, 48, 49, 78, 95, 98, 99, 100, 103, 120, 123, 130; Rachel Donelson, 14, 19
Jones: Anson, 57, 58, 72, 74, 75, 77, 92, 100, 102, 129, 130, 138, 142, 156; Thomas, 8
La Bahia, 55
Lamar: Mirabeau B., 69, 72, 77, 83, 84, 90, 91, 101, 123, 133, 136, 138, 144, 155
Lapham: Moses, 126
Lavaca, 70
law library, 36, 53, 102
Lewis: Washington, 67; William B., 22, 29, 39

Liberty: (ship), 114
Manuel Fernández Castrillón, 85
Martin Clow & Company, 76
Mason: Abram, 10; Elizabeth Brownlee, 10
Matagorda, 53, 55, 56, 70, 95, 116, 130
Matamoras, 70
McKinney: Thomas F., 69, 72, 102, 111, 113, 114, 145, 148, 149, 150, 152
McKinney & Williams, 69, 72
McLean: John, 33
Menard: Michel B., 67, 114
Merino sheep, 9
Milam: Benjamin Rush, 55, 59
Millard: Henry, 84, 123
Monmouth Court House, 2
Moore: Francis, 129
Morehouse: Edwin, 120, 122
Moreland: Isaac, 86
Nash: Joseph, 18
Nashville Inn, 13, 25
Navidad, 121, 127
New York, 19, 35, 57, 82, 86, 88, 99, 118, 127, 137, 139
Newell: Stewart, 135
Overton: John, 12
Patterson: Matthew, 7
Patton: William H., 125
Perkins: N. T., 7
Peterson: Floride, 156
Peyton: Balie, 17
Philosophical Society of Texas, 132
Pocket: (ship), 81
Polk: James K., 13
Porter: Parry Washington, 44; Thomas Jefferson, 44
Potter: Robert, 62, 66, 77, 78
Power: James, 66, 67, 146, 151
Queen Victoria, 9
Quimper: Yancey, 137
Raguet: Henry, 82
Richmond, 33, 62, 66, 81, 126, 127, 128
Rio Grande, 74, 86, 89, 110, 114, 116, 117
Robertson: James, 3; Sterling C., 77
Ross: Reuben, 43
Ross Concession, 43, 44, 45, 129
Rucks: James, 27, 30
Runaway Scrape, 66, 73
Rush: Richard, 19
Rusk: Thomas J., 66, 67, 69, 70, 72, 73, 74, 81, 83, 84, 85, 87, 88, 102, 132, 136, 155
Russell: W. J., 57
Sabine, 66, 81, 110, 114, 116, 117
San Antonio, 54, 55, 59, 67, 112, 113, 116, 117, 126, 127, 131
San Jacinto, 57, 66, 72, 74, 82, 83, 85, 87, 88, 90, 91, 101, 102, 110, 113, 126, 130, 131, 142, 156, 157
Santa Anna, 54, 59, 65, 66, 67, 70, 71, 81, 82, 83, 84, 86, 88, 89, 90, 91, 96, 101, 110, 112, 129
Saunders: David M., 14, 15, 16
Scott: Wm. J., 145
Shelby: Isaac, 39
Sherman: Sidney, 83, 84
Smith: Ashbel, 135; Erasmus "Deaf", 82, 84; Henry, 56, 67, 101
Somervell: Alexander, 84
Stewart: Charles, 71
Stock Place, 9
Summers: William W., 86
Sylvester: J. A., 86
Temple Lodge, No. 4, Ancient York Masons, 143
Terrell: W. W., 155
Texas Railroad, Navigation and Banking Company, 109, 110, 128, 129, 150
Thomas: David, 63, 66, 67, 72
Thompson: Alice, 4, 5, 7; James, 4; John, 7; Robert, 2, 7, 9, 13

Tiki Island, 140
Tompkins: A. M., 143
Townes: Robert J., 145
Travis: William Barret, 59, 65, 66, 70, 71, 130
Treaty of Velasco, 89
Tulip Grove, 9
Twin Sisters, 81
U.S. Military Academy at West Point, 14, 35, 139
Valley Forge, 2, 8
Van Buren: Martin, 24, 30, 31, 37
Velasco, 45, 53, 87, 88, 89, 90, 92, 95, 96, 97, 101, 102, 106, 110, 113, 120, 127, 128, 130, 131
Waller: Edwin, 56, 58, 62, 145
Washington: George, 2, 7, 8, 156; William, 17
Washington-on-the-Brazos, 59
Webster: Daniel, 96
Wells: Lysander, 84
Wevell: Arthur A., 43
Wharton: John A., 87, 90, 101, 127, 130; William H., 102, 109, 112
White: Walter C., 126, 127
Williams: Samuel May, 114
Wilson: Robert, 144, 149
Wood: William, 84
Wycliffe: Charles, 41
Yellow Stone: *(ship)*, 81, 88
Yoakum: Henderson King, 142
Zavala: Lorenzo de, 72, 86